LEARN ENGLISH WITH THE BIBLE

Published by Redemption Press Express, an imprint of Redemption Press, PO Box 427, Enumclaw, WA 98022. Toll-Free (844) 2REDEEM (273-3336)

Redemption Press Express is honored to present this title in partnership with the author. The views expressed or implied in this work are those of the author. Redemption Press Express provides our imprint seal representing design excellence, creative content, and high-quality production.

Your purchase of this book helps support LearnEnglishwiththeBible.com, providing more Bible-based English and ESL learning materials for teachers and English learners worldwide.

Printed in the United States of America
First Edition 2023
ISBN (print): 979-8-9880411-0-8
ISBN (ebook): 979-8-9880411-1-5

Library of Congress Catalog Number: 2023923046

Cover and interior design by Blue Ridge Graphic Design

For more information or permissions, write to:

Learn English with the Bible
P. O. Box 843
Bealeton, VA 22712
Sharon@LearnEnglishwiththeBible.com

The Story of Easter

20 Bible-Based ESL Lesson Plans

Focus on Prepositions

Sharon Rubel

Don't be afraid! I know you are looking for Jesus, who was nailed to a cross. He isn't here! God has raised him to life, just as Jesus said he would.

Matthew 28:5–6

⋟ Table of Contents ⋞

⇜ Worksheets, Games, and Quizzes ⇝

❧ Introduction ❧

Thank you so much for purchasing this curriculum guide and helping to support the ministry of Learn English with the Bible. I pray this set of lesson plans will be helpful to you as you seek to share Christ with the English learners entrusted to you.

With this book, you can share with your students the story that is the heart of Christianity: the resurrection of Jesus. I encourage you to visit LearnEnglishwiththeBible.com for more articles and lessons you can use.

English has become the language of the world. These lessons will provide your students with courses they enjoy and you with lesson plans that are easy to teach. You and your students are in my prayers every day.

In Christ,

Sharon

Sharon@LearnEnglishwiththeBible.com

❧ How to Use These Lesson Plans ❧

This book contains twenty lesson plans covering the last few days of Jesus' life on earth and his resurrection. The main Scripture passages are from Matthew 26, 27, and 28. All Bible quotations are from the Contemporary English Version (CEV).

Two-Hour Classes

There is enough material in each lesson to give you two hours of class time. If your students can't devote that much time to English, or if your own time is limited, focus on the listening, speaking, and vocabulary sections. You could also break the material into two sessions.

Adult language students tend to enjoy grammar because it is factual and they can understand it in a logical way. Speaking is more difficult, but much more useful.

Encourage Them to Speak

It's important for students to feel comfortable asking questions and sharing their insights about the gospel as they hear it taught. Encourage your students to ask a lot of questions, preferably in English. And ask plenty of questions yourself!

On the first day of class, they may not volunteer answers readily, but if you persist in asking questions, students who are hesitant to speak will be encouraged to try. If you call on students who are outgoing, this will help the rest feel more comfortable and accepted as they speak in English.

Icebreaker activities are important to help your students get to know each other. As they make friends with the other students, they will feel more comfortable coming to class each week and sharing their answers, even if they are afraid to make mistakes.

Give Students Ownership

Encourage your learners to figure things out on their own, with a minimum of input from you. For example, give a brief explanation of one grammar point, then write two sentences on the board and ask them which one is incorrect and why. This form of learning helps students remember what they have just learned. It also keeps them alert during class.

Reading Out Loud

The lessons are designed for you to read the text out loud to the students during the listening exercises. However, you can use the online audio version of the CEV Bible, read with a neutral American accent. Go to cev.bible, click on the Read link at the top of the page, navigate to the verses you need, then click the Play arrow at the bottom of the page.

Work in Pairs or Small Groups

Have your students work in pairs or small groups to complete activities and to check each other's work. This provides a number of benefits. One, it provides more chances for everyone to speak. (Be sure to monitor them and make sure they are speaking English.) Two, it allows more natural communication to happen. And finally, it gives the students a chance to learn from one another.

Bring a Notebook and Pen

Encourage your students to bring paper and pen and take notes. You may wish to have sheets of paper and pens available in case they forget.

Taking notes is helpful in many ways. The act of writing, either in English or in their own language, keeps them alert and helps them remember what they are learning. It also gives them more ownership in the class and helps them engage actively with the exercises.

Focus on Learning English

These lessons are mostly focused on learning English, rather than Bible study, since ESL could be the hook to draw people to your Christian organization. I've included some discussion questions, but at any time during the classes I encourage you to follow the Spirit's leading and engage in more gospel content as your learners ask questions or seem ready for it.

Teaching Vocabulary

A vocabulary exercise comes after each listening exercise, instead of before, to help students learn how to discover the meaning of a word from its context as they listen. This is how they will normally learn new vocabulary in everyday life. Then we teach vocabulary before the student reviews the text in the reading exercise.

There's so much more to talk about, but you will learn what works best for you. There are many online resources to help you with general classroom management. If you need to brush up on your own grammar, you'll find articles online, including at LearnEnglishwiththeBible.com. If you have questions, please don't hesitate to contact me. My email address is sharon@LearnEnglishwiththeBible. com.

On to the lessons!

The Story of Easter

Lesson 1

The Plot to Kill Jesus

When Jesus had finished teaching, he told his disciples, "You know two days from now will be Passover. This is when the Son of Man will be handed over to his enemies and nailed to a cross."

At that time the chief priests and the nation's leaders were meeting at the home of Caiaphas the high priest. They planned how they could sneak around and have Jesus arrested and put to death. But they said, "We must not do it during Passover, because the people will riot." (Matthew 26:1–5)

Introduction and Icebreaker

5–10 minutes

This activity is especially important if this is your first class meeting and your students don't know one another. This is the only icebreaker included in this book, but feel free to include an icebreaker of your choice before other lessons too.

First, introduce yourself. Write your name on the board, then tell the students:

- Your current city of residence or where you come from
- People in your immediate family (e.g., "I am married and have one daughter.")
- What languages you speak

Have students take turns introducing themselves to the group by answering the same questions. They will be more willing to speak and participate if they feel comfortable with their classmates. When they work in small groups, they will begin to trust their classmates.

Introduce the Lesson

5–7 minutes

This section contains discussion questions that are intended to introduce your students to the topic of the lesson and prepare them for what they will hear and read. There are discussion questions at the beginning of each lesson.

Since you had an icebreaker today, you might want to keep this section short. Use some or all of the questions. Write the questions on the board so students can read them along with you as you read them out loud. Ask for volunteers to answer the questions.

- Do you like to make plans, or do you like to try different things and see what happens?
- Who do you like to share your plans with? Your family? Your friends?

Write these four questions on the board before you read the Bible passage quoted at the beginning of this lesson so students have an idea of what they are about to hear and have specific details to listen for.

- How many days was it until Passover? (two)
- Who would the Son of Man be handed over to? (his enemies)
- Where were the leaders and the chief priests meeting? (at the home of Caiaphas the high priest)
- What did they want to do to Jesus? (arrest him/put him to death)

Read the passage to the students. Read at normal speed—not too slow or too fast. They should listen for the answers to the comprehension questions. Read it again, but no more than three times. Let volunteers answer the questions.

Review the vocabulary words listed below. One at a time, write each word on the board. Say it, and have students repeat after you. Write the definition. If you have beginners in your class, pictures and gestures can be very helpful.

Talk about how the word is pronounced. Say the word slowly with extra stress on the accented syllable. Ask the students if they can tell which syllable is stressed. On the board, write the word divided into syllables and mark the syllable that gets stress. Repeat the word, then have students repeat also.

Write a sample verse or two from the passage, read it, and have the students repeat it. Check their pronunciation and make gentle corrections. However, try not to call out individual students who are making mistakes. Choose a mistake that many students seem to be making, and correct it as a group. Keep them talking!

Teacher Tip

Pronunciation is noted here and in most modern dictionaries using the IPA (International Phonetic Alphabet). Learn more about the IPA at www.internationalphoneticalphabet.org.

You may or may not choose to teach students this alphabet. It can be useful for students whose native language does not use the Roman alphabet, and also for languages like English, where one letter can make several sounds.

Learn more about teaching with the IPA at https://bit.ly/LearnEnglishwiththeBibleTeachIPA.

1. Passover
(proper noun)–a Jewish festival in memory of the Jews' escape from slavery in Egypt
/ˈpæs oʊ vɚ/

"This is the **Passover** Festival in honor of me, your Lord." (Exodus 12:11)
"You and your children must continue to celebrate **Passover** each year." (Exodus 12:24–25)

2. hand over
(phrasal verb)–to formally give something to someone
/ˈhænd ˈoʊ vɚ/

"The Son of Man will be **handed over** to people who will kill him."
(Matthew 17: 22–23)

"David asked, 'Would the leaders of Keilah **hand** me and my soldiers **over** to Saul?'" (1 Samuel 23:12)

3. nail
(verb)–to join two things with a short piece of metal (also called a "nail")
/**neɪl**/

"**Nail** it down so it won't fall over." (Jeremiah 10:4)

"They will beat him and **nail** him to a cross." (Matthew 20:19)

4. sneak
(verb)–to go somewhere secretly, to avoid being seen
/**sniːk**/

"Why did you **sneak** away without telling me?" (Genesis 31:27)

"David **sneaked** over and cut off a small piece of Saul's robe, but Saul didn't notice a thing." (1 Samuel 24:4)

(The expression "a thing" is covered in the vocabulary section of lesson 12.)

5. arrest
(verb)–when police or another authority takes a person into custody because they believe that person may have committed a crime
/ə ˈ**rest**/

"He will **arrest** us, make us his slaves, and take our donkeys." (Genesis 43:18)

"The next morning, Saul sent guards to **arrest** David." (1 Samuel 19:14)

6. riot
(verb)–when a crowd of people begins to act in a violent way in a public place (can also be a noun)
/ˈ**raɪ** ət/

"We caught this man trying to get our people to **riot**." (Luke 23:2)

"The people were about to kill Paul when the Roman army commander heard that all Jerusalem was starting to **riot**." (Acts 21:31)

Now that you have discussed some of the vocabulary words, give each student a copy of the Bible passage written on paper. Let them read it quietly to themselves for a minute or so.

> **Reading**
> 5–10 minutes

Read the passage to the students while they read along. Read slowly if you need to. Read it again, then a third time if the students want you to. Ask if there are any questions about any of the words or expressions.

In the speaking sections, we'll start with simple repetition exercises. In future lessons, speaking activities will provide more variety as students become more comfortable with your class and their classmates.

Read the Bible passage a few words at a time and have students repeat after you. Go slowly the first time, then repeat, then try once at regular speed. You can add some discussion questions if you feel your students are ready to do more speaking together. Try these questions to start:

- Do you know much about how Passover is celebrated by Jewish people? (You may wish to briefly tell the story from Exodus 12:24–27.)
- Do these Jewish leaders seem like people you would want to be your leaders? Why or why not?

Consonant Clusters

English is very consonant heavy. Many times, consonants appear in strings of two, three, even four in a row. This is particularly mind-numbing for students whose native language contains more vowels. For example, native Chinese speakers tend to leave off the final consonant of an English word or simplify consonant clusters.

The *ld* Consonant Cluster

One cluster we can focus on today is the *ld* sound, found at the end of *told* and *nailed*, both included in today's text. First, practice the *l* sound by itself.

The *l* Sound

Work with your students to pronounce the *l* sound by lowering the tongue in the back of the mouth and putting the tip of the tongue on the roof of the mouth behind the front teeth (the alveolar ridge). Then use the vocal cords to produce the sound. Demonstrate for them and have them repeat.

Write the following *l* words from the passage on the board, demonstrate how they are pronounced, and help your students practice them:

disciple, will, leaders, plan

The *d* Sound

Now let's work on the *d* sound. First, the air is blocked by the tongue touching the alveolar ridge (behind the top front teeth, though the exact location can vary by region). The mouth is partially open. When you drop the tip of your tongue, you will use your vocal cords and push out a little air, and your mouth will drop open a little bit more.

Write the following words on the board, demonstrate their pronunciation, and help students say them:

had, disciple, days, handed, around

Teacher Tip

Having students repeat after you helps them learn English intonation and stress patterns. This will increase their confidence as they speak.

Pronouncing *ld*

When you put these sounds together, both sounds need to be pronounced completely. When you transition from the *l* to the *d*, the back of the tongue goes up at the same time as the rest of the tongue blocks the flow of air by quickly touching the teeth on all sides. Then the tip of the tongue comes down to pronounce the *d*.

Write the following words on the board, demonstrate their pronunciation, and ask students to repeat after you:

told, nailed, build, child, fold

Using *ld* Words in Sentences

Ask students to say the above words in sentences. Use these sample sentences or make up your own. You may write the sentences on the board or do the exercises orally.

- Jesus told the people a story.
- I nailed the shelf to the wall.
- I need to build a new house.
- The child ate a good dinner.
- Will you please fold the laundry for me?

Say the complete sentence first, then repeat more slowly in sections of three or four words as students repeat after you. Then try having the students shadow you, saying the words with you as you speak.

Spelling
5–7 minutes

Spelling is important in English and can be very challenging for English learners. However, if you are short on time, feel free to skip the spelling sections to focus more on sections you feel are more practical for your class. You can also check students' spelling during the writing exercises.

In this lesson, we'll introduce the spelling exercise with a simple dictation activity. Ask the students to get out paper and a pen. Dictate the vocabulary words one at a time and ask students to write them.

Passover, hand over, nail, sneak, arrest, riot

Put students in pairs and have them compare their answers with each other. They can make any necessary corrections when they see how their partners spelled the word. After a couple of minutes, write the words on the board and let students check their work.

Grammar
20 minutes

In each lesson of this book, we will cover one grammar topic that is found in the Bible passage. This book focuses on prepositions, a good topic for lower-intermediate and intermediate learners. In this lesson, the passage lends itself very well to a discussion of the future simple tense.

The Future Simple Tense

Write these phrases from today's lesson on the board and tell the students that these phrases contain examples of the future simple tense:

- You know two days from now **will be** Passover.
- The Son of Man **will be** handed over to his enemies.
- The people **will riot**.

Tell your students that the future simple tense is very easy to form, and it's also easy to know when to use it.

When to Use the Future Simple Tense

We use this tense to describe things that haven't happened yet. These are actions that begin and end in the future.

- I **will go** to work tomorrow.
- Peter **will arrive** next week.
- They **will be** late.

How to Form the Future Simple Tense

The future simple tense is a compound tense, meaning it needs a main verb and a helping verb. In the future simple tense, the helping verb is *will*. The main verb is used in its infinitive form. One of the easiest things about the future simple tense is that it is the same for all subjects. Write these phrases on the board as examples of how to form the future simple tense.

- I **will go**.
- You **will go**.
- He/she/it **will go**.
- We **will go**.
- They **will go**.

Ask for a few volunteers to give you an action verb, like *eat* or *work*. Write it on the board, then ask students to help you write a simple sentence around it in the present simple tense. For example, if a student suggests the verb *walk*, write it on the board. Then students might suggest:

- I **walk** to work.

Ask the students if they know how to make this sentence into the future simple tense. If nobody can answer, write the word *will* in front of the verb *walk*.

- I **will walk** to work.

Try another one:

- I **listen** in English class.
- I **will listen** in English class.

Ask your students to suggest at least three more sentences, first suggesting a verb, then suggesting a simple sentence using that verb. Wait patiently to see if the students can make suggestions. If you have a quiet class, you may need to suggest verbs and write sentences yourself at first.

Contractions Are Important

Verb tenses that use helping verbs, like the future simple tense, will normally be made into contractions while speaking. See if you have a volunteer who can explain to the class what a contraction is.

Ask for another volunteer to help you change the first sentence to a contraction, attaching the subject to the helping verb *will* by changing *will* to "apostrophe + *ll*." Write a new sentence, because you will need your original sentences for the next parts of the lesson.

- I **will walk** to work.
- **I'll walk** to work.

Now change the rest of the sentences that students suggested into contractions. If you like, write the following extra sentences on the board for practice with different subjects. Ask the class to help you make contractions.

- You will pick me up, right? (You'll)
- He will catch the bus. (He'll catch/She'll catch)
- It will be okay. (It'll—students may need help with this pronunciation)
- We will be late. (We'll)
- They will fix the car. (They'll)

Making the Future Simple Tense Negative

Erase the contracted sentences and ask if anyone knows how to change the original future simple sentences into negative sentences. If nobody knows, tell them to insert *not* after the word *will*. Demonstrate with the original sentences:

- I **will not walk** to work.
- I **will not listen** in English class.

Ask your students to help you change all the sentences on the board into negative sentences.

Contractions Are Important

In a negative sentence, we generally contract the words *will* and *not* together, making *won't*. Write new sentences, changing the first *will not* sentence into a contraction to show students how this works. Then ask them to help you change

Except for the present simple and the past simple, the twelve English verb tenses are compound verbs. All compound verbs are made negative by putting *not* after the first helping verb.

Present Tense

I travel.
I am not traveling.
I have not traveled.
I have not been traveling.

Past Tense

I traveled.
I was not traveling.
I had not traveled.
I had not been traveling.

Future Tense

I will not travel.
I will not be traveling.
I will not have traveled.
I will not have been traveling.

This teacher tip is for your use and does not need to be shared with your students at this level.

the rest of the *will not* sentences to *won't*. Use the sentences that students suggested first, then the simple sentences with all subjects. Help students notice that the verb does not change according to the subject used.

- I **won't walk** to work.
- I **won't listen** in English class.
- You **won't pick** me **up**, right?
- He **won't catch** the bus.
- It **won't be** okay.
- We **won't be** late.
- They **won't fix** the car.

Making a Question with the Future Simple Tense

Change all the sentences on the board into questions. See if any of the students can help you do this. If not, tell them that to make a question in the future simple, reverse the order of the subject and the helping verb.

Teacher Tip
Contractions are not normally used with basic questions in the future simple tense.

- **Will** I **walk** to work?
- **Will** I **listen** in English class?

Do this with all the sentences students suggested, and the extra sentences with other subjects if you have used them.

- **Will** you **pick** me **up**?
- **Will** he **catch** the bus?
- **Will** it **be** okay?
- **Will** we **be** late?
- **Will** they **fix** the car?

The Future Simple Tense with *Going To*

No discussion of the future simple tense in English would be complete without a discussion of the words/phrases *am/is/are going to*. This is very common in both speech and writing, and your students have probably heard it before. Just remind them that it is informal.

With the subject at the beginning of the sentence, add the verb *be* conjugated to match the subject, then change *will* to *going to*. Change the first sentence, then ask students to help you change the rest. Use contractions because they are very common and almost always used in casual speech.

- I**'m going to walk** to work. (I am going to)
- I**'m going to listen** in English class. (I am going to)
- You**'re going to pick** me **up**, right? (You are going to)
- He**'s going to** catch the bus. (He is going to)
- It**'s going to** be okay. (It is going to)

- We're **going to be** late. (We are going to)
- They're **going to fix** the car. (They are going to)

Have students repeat these sentences after you, several times if necessary. You may also want to include a discussion of the American English pronunciation of *going to—gonna.*

- I'm **gonna walk** to work. (I am going to)
- I'm **gonna listen** in English class. (I am going to)
- You're **gonna pick** me **up**, right? (You are going to)
- He's **gonna catch** the bus. (He is going to)
- It's **gonna be** okay. (It is going to)
- We're **gonna be** late. (We are going to)
- They're **gonna fix** the car. (They are going to)

It's important to mention to students that *gonna* is only for speaking. In writing, they should always use *going to,* never *gonna.*

Remind them that they can use *will, going to, or gonna* when they speak and they will be understood. But they may find that they will sound the most native when they use *gonna* as their future simple word of choice. Whatever they choose to say, they need to understand what they are hearing when someone says *gonna.*

Let's see how well the students recall the vocabulary words they learned earlier in the lesson. Again, you may choose not to use the writing exercises if your time is limited. I find, though, that most English learners are very hesitant to write. Ask them to compose simple sentences with the vocabulary and grammar they have just learned. This will help cement the lesson in their memory and help them be more confident in their writing skills.

For today's writing practice, write the vocabulary words on the board again and ask students to compose two sentences in their notebooks. Each sentence should contain at least one of the vocabulary words and, if possible, use the future simple tense. Then ask for volunteers to come up to the board and share their sentences with the class. Note everything they did right, then gently ask if you may make corrections to their sentences. Correct any grammatical or spelling errors and encourage them generously.

Writing

10–15 minutes

That's the end of the first lesson!

I've only included language lessons, but at any time during any lesson you could include some discussion of the Bible verses and what they mean. Here are a few sample questions for lesson 1:

- Why did the Sanhedrin think the people would riot if they knew Jesus had been arrested?
- What do you think about the actions of the Sanhedrin, meeting secretly in a home?
- How could Jesus predict what would happen to him in two days?
- Why was it part of God's plan for Jesus to die on a cross?
- Any other comments or thoughts?

You may not get much response since this involves speaking in English and it's just the first class, but it's worth a try. If you write the questions on the board, the students may copy them into their notebooks (probably in their own language) and think about them later.

Do whichever parts of the lesson you feel are most important, or that you have time for, and skip other parts. You could divide the lesson into two lessons if that works best. This curriculum is just a guide for you, though your students will benefit from exercises in the four major skills—reading, listening, speaking, and writing—as well as practice in vocabulary, grammar, spelling, and pronunciation.

The Story of Easter

Lesson 2

At Bethany

Jesus was in the town of Bethany, eating at the home of Simon, who had leprosy. A woman came in with a bottle of expensive perfume and poured it on Jesus' head. But when his disciples saw this, they became angry and complained, "Why such a waste? We could have sold this perfume for a lot of money and given it to the poor."

Jesus knew what they were thinking, and he said:

Why are you bothering this woman? She has done a beautiful thing for me. You will always have the poor with you, but you won't always have me. She has poured perfume on my body to prepare it for burial. You may be sure that wherever the good news is told all over the world, people will remember what she has done. And they will tell others. (Matthew 26:6–13)

Introduce the Lesson
5–10 minutes

Use any or all of the following questions or write your own. Write the questions on the board so the students can read them as you ask them out loud and refer back to them while they think of their answers.

- Do you like perfume? Do you wear perfume or cologne?
- If you heard a wonderful story, would you tell others?
- Have you ever read a good story on social media and shared it? What was the story about?

Listening Comprehension
10–15 minutes

Write the following questions on the board before you read today's text so students will have an idea of what they are about to hear and have specific information to listen for.

- What town was Jesus in? (Bethany)
- What was he doing? (eating)
- Who was he eating with? (his disciples and Simon)
- Who came in with a bottle of perfume? (a woman)

Now read the Bible passage to the students. They should listen for the answers to the comprehension questions. Read it again, but no more than three times. Ask for volunteers to answer the questions.

Vocabulary

10–15 minutes

This lesson has very easy vocabulary, but we'll look at five of the words. First, write the vocabulary word on the board, say it, and write the definition. If you have beginners in your class, pictures and gestures can be very helpful.

Talk about how each word is pronounced. Say it slowly, with extra stress on the accented syllable. Ask the students if they can tell which syllable is stressed. Then write it on the board, separating the syllables, and mark the syllable that gets stress.

Write a sample verse or two, read it, and have the students repeat it. Check their pronunciation and make gentle corrections. Keep them talking!

Teacher Tip

Notice that the IPA pronunciation of *pour* and *poor* is different. Often they are both pronounced as /pɔːr/.

1. pour
(verb)–to make a liquid or other substance flow from a container in a continuous stream
/pɔːr/

"He **poured** olive oil on the rock to dedicate it to God." (Genesis 28:18)

"No one **pours** new wine into old wineskins." (Matthew 9:17)

2. poor
(adjective)–having very little money
/pʊr/

"Even the **poor** will eat until they are full." (Psalm 132:15)

"The rich think highly of themselves, but anyone **poor** and sensible sees right through them." (Proverbs 28:11)

3. waste
(verb)–to use something in a careless or unnecessary way
/weɪst/

"My friends, you know our time with you wasn't **wasted**." (1 Thessalonians 2:1)

"So when they came here with me, I **wasted** no time." (Acts 25:17)

4. bother
(verb)–to annoy, worry, or upset someone
/ˈbɑːðɚ/

"Your daughter has died. Why **bother** the teacher anymore?" (Mark 5:35)

"I don't want to **bother** you, but please be patient with us and listen to me for just a few minutes." (Acts 24:4)

5. world

(noun)–the earth, with all its countries, peoples and natural features

/wɜːld/

"Solomon was the richest and wisest king in the **world**." (2 Chronicles 9:22)

"Our Lord, your love is seen all over the **world**." (Psalm 119:64)

Ask if there are any other words the students want you to define for them.

Hand out the Bible passage written on paper. Let the students read silently for two minutes. Next, read it slowly out loud for the students as they follow along silently. Read a second time. If they need you to read it again, do so. Ask if there are any questions about anything.

Reading

5–10 minutes

Read the passage a few words at a time, and have the students repeat the words out loud after you. Go slowly the first time, then again, then a couple of times at regular speed. This helps with pronunciation and confidence. Then try shadowing, where the students say the verse with you at the same time. This is more difficult, but it will help with pronunciation and confidence as well as with learning rhythm and intonation.

Speaking

5–7 minutes

To help students put their thoughts into words, here are two questions for discussion:

- Do you sometimes worry about wasting your time or possessions? What does it mean to be *generous*?
- How can you be more generous with your time, money, or possessions? Do you think that is something God wants us to do?

When you do a classroom discussion like this as a speaking exercise, don't correct students' mistakes unless they ask you to. The purpose of an exercise like this is to help them feel comfortable and confident when they speak in English. If they are making themselves understood, they are communicating well.

Pronouncing Prepositions

In today's grammar lesson, we will begin to cover prepositions. In this pronunciation section, let's talk more about how to pronounce these prepositions, because it isn't always as easy as it seems.

Pronunciation

20 minutes

Stressed and Unstressed Words and Syllables

English pronunciation depends a lot on stressed and unstressed words and syllables. Words that get stress are usually content words that give the sentence meaning, like nouns, verbs, adjectives, and adverbs. Words that give structure to the sentence (pronouns, prepositions, conjunctions, and articles) are usually not

We'll talk about the schwa sound in a future lesson. Schwa will unlock your students' ability to understand spoken English.

Schwa comes from Hebrew. It was first used as a linguistic term in Germany in the 1800s. Many native English speakers are unaware of their use of this sound, though it is considered to be the most common sound in the English language.

The use of the schwa sound will vary in all the different accents of English spoken around the world.

Learn more about schwa at LearnEnglish-withtheBible.com, "How to Pronounce the Schwa Sound in American English."

stressed. Very often the pronunciation of these structure words changes according to the words around them.

We call this "reducing" a word. The word is still there, but it is pronounced softly and quickly. The prepositions *on, in,* and *at* are excellent examples of this. When students learn these words, they are taught the dictionary pronunciation. But when native speakers pronounce these words in sentences, they are barely recognizable to an English learner.

Stressed Words

Write this sample sentence on the board:

- Jesus was in the town of Bethany, eating at the home of Simon, who had leprosy.

Highlight the stressed content words:

- **Jesus** was in the **town** of **Bethany, eating** at the **home** of **Simon,** who had **leprosy.**

Say the sentence for the class. Ask them to notice the stress you are putting on the content words, and how the structure words are said quickly and quietly. Let them repeat after you a few times.

Explain that English is very rhythmic. Ask the students if they have noticed this. Native speakers will unconsciously put the same amount of time between each stressed word, regardless of how many unstressed words come between the stressed ones. That's the reason unstressed words are reduced—to try to keep the same gap of time between each stressed word.

Unstressed Words

The prepositions in our sentence—*in, at,* and *of*—are the poor losers in this musical game. These structure words are not stressed, so the pronunciation becomes incomplete. *In* becomes *n, at* becomes *a* (stopping the consonant *t* without pronouncing it fully), and *of* becomes *v.*

Try it! Say the sentence at normal speed and listen to how the vowels change. If you do say the unstressed vowel, chances are that it morphs into a schwa, or *uh* sound.

As you explain this to your students, say the sentence at a normal speed and have them listen carefully to how the vowels change. Then have them repeat after you several times. They don't have to get it perfect, because this is something they will learn more completely as they practice their listening and speaking skills.

You can tell them they don't need to pronounce words this way, because they will always be understood if they use the dictionary pronunciation. But if they are hoping to sound more like a native speaker, they should practice reducing words by listening and repeating. Even if they don't want to learn to speak this way, this knowledge is important for them as they listen to English.

Erase everything written on the board. Then ask students to get out a a pen and paper. Dictate the five vocabulary words to the students. For a bonus point, ask them to create a sentence with that word, making a total of 10 possible points.

Students can pair up and exchange papers to check each other's work. See who earned the most points, and let a few volunteers write a sentence on the board to check grammar.

Three Prepositions of Location: *In, On,* and *At*

Learning prepositions gives language learners all over the world a massive headache, not just those learning English. Luckily, we can identify several guidelines involving *in, on,* and *at* when we use them to talk about where something is.

In general, here are the definitions for these prepositions when we are describing the location of something:

> **in:** indicating position within an enclosed space
> **on:** indicating position upon the surface of something
> (not necessarily horizontal)
> **at:** indicating position related to an exact place or point

In

Write the definition for *in* on the board. Then write the following verses on the board one at a time and ask students to explain why the preposition *in* needs to be used. What "enclosed space" is being referred to in each sentence?

- Jesus was **in** the town of Bethany.
- "Sir, I don't have anyone to put me **in** the pool when the water is stirred up." (John 5:7)
- "Paul asked to be kept **in** jail." (Acts 25:21)

On

Write the definition for *on* and the following sample verses. Ask why the word *on* fits in these sentences. What "surface" is being referred to in each sentence?

- She poured it on Jesus' head.
- She has poured perfume on my body.
- "Don't you put a lamp on a lampstand?" (Mark 4:21)

At

Write the definition for *at* and the following sample verses. Ask why we need the preposition *at* in these sentences. What "place or point" is being referred to in these sentences or phrases?

- ... eating at the home of Simon ("in" could also be used)
- He "broke them to pieces at the foot of the mountain." (Exodus 32:19)
- "God put winged creatures at the entrance to the garden." (Genesis 3:24)

Spelling

5–8 minutes

Grammar

20 minutes

Teacher Tip

In, on, and *at* are required by certain verbs, but this is purely grammatical and is one reason prepositions can be so confusing. For example, you can "laugh at" something, but you won't "laugh in" or "laugh on."

Prepositions are used in different ways in different languages. For example, in English you would go "to" Italy, but in Italian you go "in" Italy ("in Italia").

Teaching prepositions requires repetition with lots of examples so students can learn how they are used in English.

Teacher Tip

If students ask you about the difference between *in* and *into*, the answer is that *into* implies movement. You move "into" a place vs. already being "in" that place.

Usage is similar for *on* and *onto. Onto* implies movement, and *on* usually describes location, though it can sometimes refer to movement.

Other Prepositions of Location

There are other prepositions that can describe the location of something. You have to be careful, though, because prepositions can also be used as other parts of speech. For example, you can say:

- The cat is **outside**. (adverb)
- The cat is **outside** the house. (preposition)
- Just drive **by**; don't stop. (adverb)
- They live in the house **by** the river. (preposition)

In general, when a word is being used as a preposition, it will be followed by a noun that may or may not have an article (*a, an, the*) with it. This is a prepositional phrase: preposition + object.

Prepositional Phrases

A preposition is always part of a prepositional phrase. Prepositional phrases are used to add descriptive information to the sentence, but they are not usually necessary to make the sentence grammatically correct. Write the following sentence on the board, and have students help you identify the prepositions of location:

- Jesus was **in** the town of Bethany, eating **at** the home of Simon, who had leprosy.

Now ask them to tell you the noun that comes after each of the following prepositions:

- in **the town**
- at **the home**

If we take all the prepositional phrases and other clauses out of the sentence (including the prepositional phrases that start with the preposition *of*), we are still left with a grammatically correct sentence:

- Jesus was ~~in the town of Bethany,~~ eating ~~at the home of Simon, who had leprosy.~~
- Jesus was eating.

The verb phrase *was eating* is in the past continuous tense, and this tense is usually used for giving us background information. Because of this, our sentence "Jesus was eating" seems incomplete. The prepositional phrases give us this extra information. The entire sentence, in the past continuous tense, sets the stage for what happens next in the story.

Teacher Tip

The phrase "who had leprosy" is called a relative clause. This is not a prepositional phrase but a clause starting with a relative pronoun like *that, who, which*, etc.

Like a prepositional phrase, a relative clause is used to add extra information to a sentence. In this sentence, it distinguishes this Simon, who had leprosy, from anyone else also named Simon.

At, In, and On in Expressions

Some expressions using *at, in,* and *on* as prepositions of location do not follow the rules. One common example is when we are using a computer or other device with a screen. What we see is "on" the screen. There are many more, like *on purpose* and *on the other hand.*

- I watched a movie **on** Netflix.
- He spends all his time **on** his phone.
- The building was **on** fire.

In and On in Phrasal Verbs

It is also common to see *in* and *on* used as part of a phrasal verb.

- move in
- give in
- count on
- hold on

Teacher Tip

You can share this information about expressions, idioms, and phrasal verbs with your students if they are more advanced or if they ask about it. But when teaching expressions, idioms, and phrasal verbs, it's best to do just one or two at a time. This is less overwhelming for students, and it helps them remember what they've learned.

Worksheet

Make a copy of Appendix A for each student. Let them work through the exercises individually, then divide into pairs and compare answers. When they have finished, call on one pair to give you the answer they agreed on. Ask the rest of the pairs if they agree. The answers are on page 2 of Appendix A.

Let's do a little writing practice with prepositions of location. Write some simple sentences on the board or ask your students to suggest some. For example:

Writing
10–15 minutes

- Mary was standing.
- John was walking.
- They were riding.
- We are sitting.
- I am hanging a picture.

Ask students to pair up with someone different than they usually choose, and as a team pick two of the sentences. Working together, they should add a prepositional phrase to each sentence, using the prepositions of location: *at, in,* and *on.* Give them three or four minutes. Some samples of correct answers would be:

- Mary was standing at the desk.
- John was walking on the sidewalk.
- They were riding in the car.
- We are sitting at the airport.
- I am hanging a picture on the wall.

Ask for volunteers to write a sentence on the board to share with the class. If the sentences are not correct, ask permission to correct them, then write your corrections as you explain them to the class. You could ask other students to help you correct any mistakes, but be cautious of the temperament of your class and the feelings of individual students.

The Story of Easter

Lesson 3

Judas and the Chief Priests

> Judas Iscariot was one of the twelve disciples. He went to the chief priests and asked, "How much will you give me if I help you arrest Jesus?" They paid Judas 30 silver coins, and from then on he started looking for a good chance to betray Jesus. (Matthew 26:14–16)

Today's text is very short, so you might want to include more discussion, or use any extra time at the end of the lesson to play a game, like Twenty Questions (see instructions in Lesson 20).

Use any or all of these introduction questions or write your own. Write them on the board so the students can read them as you ask them out loud and refer back to them while they compose their answers.

- Have you ever known somebody you didn't trust? What did that person do to make you lose trust in him or her?
- How did that make you feel?
- Do you think you would know if somebody pretended to be your friend but really wasn't?

Introduce the Lesson
5–10 minutes

Write the following comprehension questions on the board before you read the verse so students have an idea of what they are about to hear and have specific information to listen for.

- How many disciples did Jesus have? (12)
- How many silver coins did the chief priests pay Judas? (30)

Read the verse to the students several times and ask them to answer the questions based only on their listening.

Listening Comprehension
10–15 minutes

Write the word on the board, and pronounce it as you write the definition. If the word is a verb, conjugate it after you have worked through the meaning and pronunciation.

Pronounce the word once, then pronounce it a second time with exaggerated stress on the accented syllable. Ask the students if they can tell which syllable is stressed. Practice saying the word with correct stress several times, then call on individual students to say the word.

Vocabulary
10–15 minutes

Read the sample passage one verse at a time and have the students repeat after you. Correct mistakes in the pronunciation of the vocabulary words, but not the rest of the sentence unless they ask you to.

1. chief
(adjective)–the most important
/tʃiːf/

"Each of Ishmael's sons was a tribal **chief**." (Genesis 25:16)

"When Christ the **Chief** Shepherd returns ..." (1 Peter 5:4)

2. how much
(expression)–usually in the form of a question asking about the quantity of something
/haʊ mʌtʃ/

"**How much** longer will you try to have things both ways?" (1 Kings 18:21)

"Go home to your family and tell them **how much** the Lord has done for you." (Mark 5:19)

3. coins
(noun, plural)–pieces of metal stamped and endorsed by a government to use as money
(Note: *Coins* is included in the vocabulary list because of all the different ways to refer to money—money, cash, bills, change, currency, etc. You may wish to discuss these other words with your students.)
/kɔɪnz/

"These books were worth about 50,000 silver **coins**." (Acts 19:19)

"Finally, a poor widow came up and put in two **coins** worth only a few pennies." (Mark 12:42)

4. chance
(noun)–an opportunity
/tʃæns/

"Now I am going to give you one more **chance**." (Daniel 3:15)

"This will be your **chance** to tell about your faith." (Luke 21:13)

5. betray
(verb)–to deliver or expose to an enemy by treachery or disloyalty
/bɪ ˈtreɪ/

"Many will give up and will **betray** and hate each other." (Matthew 24:10)

"I have already told you what the Lord Jesus did on the night he was **betrayed**."
(1 Corinthians 11:23)

Hand out the Bible passage written on paper and let the students read it. Then read it out loud as they read along quietly to themselves. If they need you to read it again, do so. Ask if there are any questions about any of the words.

Reading
5–10 minutes

Read the Bible passage a few words at a time, and have the students repeat the words out loud after you. Go slowly the first time, then again, then a couple of times at regular speed. Correct pronunciation as necessary. Then try shadowing, where the students say the verse with you at the same time.

Ask, "What do you think about what Judas did?" Have a short discussion about the verse.

Speaking
5–7 minutes

The Sounds of C

C is an odd letter because it has no sound of its own. It could be pronounced *s*, as in *cents*, or *k*, as in *coin*. When it appears in the digraph *ch*, both of the individual sounds are lost. *Ch* even has its own IPA symbol: /tʃ/.

Pronunciation
20 minutes

Hard *C*

Students can be confused about how to know what sound *c* makes when they see it written. Usually, when *c* is followed by the vowels *a, o,* and *u,* it will have the hard *k* sound /k/. Write the following words on the board, pronounce them, and ask students to repeat after you. Then call on individual students to say the word you point to.

Iscariot

cat

coins

company

cut

cucumber

Soft *C*

When the *c* is followed by an *e* or an *i,* it usually makes the softer *s* sound /s/. Make sure students know the definition of each of the following words. Write them on the board, pronounce them, and have students repeat after you. After you have practiced, call on individual students to say the word you point to.

cents

celery

disciples

cinnamon

The /s/ and /k/ sounds are fairly common in many languages, so students should have little difficulty making them.

The *CH* Sound

When *c* is combined with the letter *h,* it makes the *ch* sound /tʃ/. To make this sound, students will round their lips, protruding slightly, then touch their tongues against the roof of their mouths on all sides, stopping the air. Slowly lowering the tip of the tongue releases a burst of air that makes the *ch* sound. Practice with the class.

If students have difficulty, ask them to pronounce the letter *t,* which is very similar except that the mouth is in a more normal position, slightly open and relaxed. Continue making the *t* sound as you round your lips and push them out, and see if they can make the sound change from *t* to *ch.* Practice saying these words from today's lesson:

> **chief**
> **much**
> **chance**

Exceptions to the Rules

These rules apply when *c* is followed by a vowel, not a consonant, as in *action.* And *ch* will make the *k* sound when it is followed by an *r,* as in *Christ* and *Christmas.* Words with irregular pronunciation will need to be learned as students encounter them.

Spelling

5–8 minutes

Choose five or six words from either the vocabulary section or the pronunciation section. Dictate them to the students as they write. Tell them you are going to say them twice at normal speed, and they will need to listen carefully. Students should exchange papers and grade each other's work as you write the words correctly on the board.

Grammar

20 minutes

Grammar Review

Ask the students to refer to the paper you gave them during the reading exercise. Ask them to find the example of the future tense ("How much will you give me ..."). It's a question, so the subject (*you*) comes between the helping verb *will* and the main verb, *give.*

The Preposition *Of*

Let's continue our discussion of prepositions by looking at a very useful one: *of.* It has many meanings, but we will illustrate a few of the most common ways it is used. The two meanings that will be most relevant to your beginning and intermediate students are:

1. Who or what does it belong to?
2. What is it made from?

1. Who or What Does It Belong To?

Write the first definition for *of* on the board, with the meaning of "Who or what does it belong to?" Write this sentence from today's text:

- Judas Iscariot was one **of** the twelve disciples.

Ask the students if Judas Iscariot was a disciple from Jesus' inner circle of twelve men. Yes, he was; therefore, he was a part *of* the group. The sentence tells us that Judas belonged to that group.

Here are some more examples. Write them on the board and ask the students how the preposition *of* is used to show who or what something belongs to.

- "Lot settled near the cities **of** the valley." (Genesis 13:12)
  The cities were all located in the valley, so they belonged to that group of cities. (The cities were also "in" the valley, but *in* has the meaning of physical location. There is a sense of belonging to a group of cities that were all together in the valley that is implied by the preposition *of.*)

- "By now there were about 5,000 followers **of** the Lord." (Acts 4:4)
  The "followers" belong to or relate to the Lord.

Using *Of* to Show Possession

We can use *of* to show that something belongs to someone or something else. This usage is used more in other languages than it is in English. But there is another common way to show who or what something belongs to in English: "apostrophe + *s.*"

Using "Apostrophe + *S*" to Show Possession

Look at these examples:

- The Son of God
- The temple of Solomon
- The house of the Lord

Explain that all of these phrases are grammatically correct, using *of* to show how one thing belongs to another. This is a more formal use, and it is seen a lot in the Bible and literary or academic writing. In casual and spoken English, however, the possessive is often made by adding an "apostrophe + *s*" at the end of the noun that is the owner.

Ask the students to help you show belonging in these phrases by deleting *the* and *of* in the sample phrases above and substituting an "apostrophe + *s.*"

Teacher Tip

It is difficult to learn how to use prepositions in a foreign language. Most English prepositions have many uses, and they may not correspond to the use of the same preposition in another language. English may use a preposition in one instance, where another language may not use one at all.

There are rules for how to use English prepositions, but there are also a lot of exceptions. The best way for your students to learn is by hearing the prepositions used in sentences again and again.

- God's Son
- Solomon's temple
- The Lord's house

Help the students understand that in their language they might say, "the doctor of my grandmother," but in English we say, "my grandmother's doctor." Provide more examples if students need more practice.

2. What Is It Made From?

A second common way we use *of* is to describe what something is made from. Look at this verse:

- "The sea had made a wall **of** water on each side **of** the Israelites." (Exodus 14:29)

The first time we see *of*, it is describing what the wall is made from. It is not being used to show belonging or relationship, because we can't say, "the water's wall." The second *of*, however, does indicate belonging. It shows how the "sides" refer to the Israelites and belong to them. The sides are not made *of* Israelites. In this one verse you can see two of the most common uses of the preposition *of*.

Here are some more examples of the preposition *of* used to show what something is made from:

- "The wall was built **of** jasper, and the city was made **of** pure gold, clear as crystal." (Revelation 21:18)

- "The crowd **of** people saw the fire and the Lord's glory." (2 Chronicles 7:3)

- "Listening to good advice is worth much more than jewelry made **of** gold." (Proverbs 25:12)

Ask the students what noun is being described with the preposition *of* in each of these verses (wall, crowd, jewelry) and what noun is being used to tell what it is made from (jasper, people, gold).

Using Nouns as Adjectives

Sometimes using *of* to describe what something is made from is necessary, as in "a crowd of people." But sometimes English speakers can get around this by using one noun to describe another noun—using a noun as an adjective. For example, instead of saying, "jewelry of gold," English speakers usually say, "gold jewelry." We have just used the noun *gold* to describe the other noun, *jewelry*.

Saying "the temple of Solomon" or "jewelry of gold" is formal and used more in writing than speaking. When speaking, it would be more common to hear "Solomon's temple" or "gold jewelry." But it takes time for English learners to understand and feel comfortable doing this themselves.

Write the following sentences on the board:

- We went to the store of shoes yesterday.
- There is an exhibition of sculpture at the museum.

Ask the students to help you get rid of the *of* and use the nouns as adjectives. Rewrite the sentences.

- We went to the shoe store yesterday.
- There is a sculpture exhibition at the museum.

More Practice with *Of*

There are many more things to say about the little word *of*. However, this is enough for one lesson, so we'll stop here.

Let's close this grammar section with a few more Bible verses using the word *of*. Ask your students how the preposition is being used in each of the following sentences.

- "His wife Elizabeth was from the family **of** Aaron." (Luke 1:5)
  (The family belonged to Aaron. You could say, "Aaron's family.")

- "A cluster **of** grapes that produces wine is worth keeping!" (Isaiah 65:8)
  (Shows what something is made of. You could say, "grape cluster.")

This week's passage is very short, so ask the students to get out a pen and paper as you dictate it to them. Read the whole passage to the students three times.

The first time, read it through at normal speed without stopping, and ask the students to listen carefully. The second time, say it slowly, phrase by phrase, as students write. The third time, say it at regular speed so students can check their work. As you read the passage, you can say things like "comma" and "period" to help students put the punctuation in the proper place.

Pair students up to check each other's work. Then ask for a volunteer or two to write their sentences on the board. Ask everyone to help you make corrections.

Writing

10–15 minutes

Teacher Tip
Some students like to write on the board, so encourage that. It gets them up and out of their seats and more engaged with the lesson.

The Story of Easter

Lesson 4

Jesus Eats the Passover Meal with His Disciples

On the first day of the Festival of Thin Bread, Jesus' disciples came to him and asked, "Where do you want us to prepare the Passover meal?"

Jesus told them to go to a certain man in the city and tell him, "Our teacher says, 'My time has come! I want to eat the Passover meal with my disciples in your home.'" They did as Jesus told them and prepared the meal.

When Jesus was eating with his twelve disciples that evening, he said, "One of you will surely hand me over to my enemies."

The disciples were very sad, and each one said to Jesus, "Lord, you can't mean me!"

He answered, "One of you men who has eaten with me from this dish will betray me. The Son of Man will die, as the Scriptures say. But it's going to be terrible for the one who betrays me! That man would be better off if he had never been born."

Judas said, "Teacher, you surely don't mean me!"

"That's what you say!" Jesus replied. But later, Judas did betray him. (Matthew 26:17–25)

Use any or all of the following conversation questions or write your own. Write them on the board so the students can read them as you ask them out loud. Refer back to them while they compose their answers.

- Do you enjoy eating special holiday meals with your family?
- Have you ever spoken the truth to someone, knowing it would make them sad?

Write the following comprehension questions on the board before you read the verses so students have an idea of what they are about to hear and have specific information to listen for.

- Jesus told the disciples to go to a certain man. Where did the man live? (in the city)
- During what part of the day did Jesus eat with his disciples? (evening)

Read the verse to the students several times and ask for volunteers to answer the questions based on their listening. Read it slowly if students ask, but try to read at a normal speed.

Write each vocabulary word on the board and pronounce it, with extra stress on the accented syllable. Ask the students if they can tell which syllable is stressed. Mark the syllable that gets stress and practice saying it again.

Write the definition and help students understand what it means. Write a sample verse or two, read it out loud, and have the students repeat it. Check their pronunciation and make gentle corrections. Have them repeat as many words and phrases after you as possible, until it gets to be a habit.

1. thin
(adjective)–having a smaller distance between opposite sides than normal; the opposite of thick
/θɪn/

"Other seeds fell on **thin**, rocky ground and quickly started growing because the soil wasn't very deep." (Matthew 13:5)

"The Festival of **Thin** Bread, also called Passover, was near." (Luke 22:1)

2. prepare
(verb)–to make something or someone ready
/prɪ ˈper/

"She **has prepared** the meat and set out the wine. Her feast is ready." (Proverbs 9:2)

"She has poured perfume on my body to **prepare** it for burial." (Matthew 26:12)

3. certain
(adjective)–mentions a particular thing or person without giving details
/ˈsɝː tən/

"You even celebrate **certain** days, months, seasons, and years." (Galatians 4:10)

"I asked you to stay on in Ephesus and warn **certain** people there to stop spreading their false teachings." (1 Timothy 1:3)

4. home

(noun)–the place you live in, especially with your family

/**hoʊm**/

"Write them [the laws] on the door frames of your **homes** and on your town gates." (Deuteronomy 11:20)

"One day, when Jacob was cooking some stew, Esau came **home** hungry." (Genesis 25:29)

5. surely

(adverb)–used to show that you are almost certain of what you are saying and want other people to agree

/ˈ**ʃʊr** li/

"If we obey the Lord, he will **surely** give us that land rich with milk and honey." (Numbers 14:8)

"As **surely** as rain blows in from the north, anger is caused by cruel words." (Proverbs 25:23)

Hand out the Scripture passage written on paper and let them read it. Then read it out loud for the students as they read along quietly to themselves. If they need you to read it again, do so. Ask if there are any questions about any of the words.

Reading
5–10 minutes

Read the verse a few words at a time, and have the students repeat the words out loud after you. Go slowly the first time, then again, then a couple of times at regular speed. Correct any pronunciation as necessary. Then try shadowing, where the students say the verse with you at the same time.

Speaking
5–7 minutes

Ask, "Why do you think Judas asked Jesus, 'Surely you can't mean me?'" Have a short discussion about the verse.

The Consonant (Vowel?) Y

Technically, the letter y is considered a semivowel. In grade school, were you taught that the vowels were *a, e, i, o, u,* and sometimes *y?*" I know I was!

Pronunciation
20 minutes

This information may help you when you try to describe the *y* sound to your students. A vowel is defined as a sound that is made with your mouth open and your tongue not touching anything. The sound is made with your vocal cords (a "voiced" sound) and shaped by your lip and jaw position. There is nothing stopping or slowing the flow of air.

A consonant is defined as a sound that is made by partially or completely stopping the flow of air by using your tongue, teeth, lips, etc. to change the sound. The letter *y* can make both of these kinds of sounds, depending on its position in the word.

Y Used as a Consonant

When *y* is at the beginning of a word, or at the beginning of a syllable, it is usually functioning as a consonant. Write the following words on the board. Demonstrate the pronunciation of *y*. It is a "moving" consonant, because your mouth will change shape as you say the letter (*ee-uh*). Pronounce these words for the class and have them repeat.

yard, yellow, beyond, lawyer

Ask students to think of other words that begin with *y* (*you, yes, yet,* etc.). Write all correct suggestions on the board, practice them, then call on students one by one to pronounce a word as you point to it.

Y Used as a Vowel

Write these words on the board:

happy, my, bicycle, cycle, system, day

Ask for a volunteer to see if they can pronounce the *y* sound in each word correctly. Explain that there are a few general rules for how to pronounce *y* when it is being used as a vowel.

Teacher Tip

You can read more about the letter y at merriam-webster.com/words-at-play/why-y-is-some-times-a-vowel-usage.[1]

1. *Y* usually sounds like long *e*.

The *y* follows the vowels *o* or *e* or a consonant at the end of a word with two or more syllables.

daily, beauty, toy, honey

If the vowel *a* is followed by a *y*, the *y* is essentially silent and allows the word to end with the long *a* pronunciation, a moving vowel which ends with the long *e* sound (*a-ee*).

way, replay, delay

2. *Y* usually sounds like long *i*.

The *y* follows a consonant at the end of a one syllable word.

fly, my, by, cry

Or if it appears in the middle of a one-syllable word.

type, rhyme

3. *Y* usually sounds like short *i*.

The *y* appears by itself in a word or a syllable with no other vowels.

myth, sym-bol, ty-pi-cal, bi-cy-cle

Practice the sample words. Students shouldn't have too much trouble with the *ee* sound, but make sure that long *i* and short *i* are being pronounced correctly. These sounds are not common in other languages.

Exceptions to the Rules

There are, of course, exceptions to these general rules. Instead of memorizing the rules, it can be more practical to learn the words one by one as students encounter them. Help your students practice the following words with *y* that appeared in our text today:

day, say, betray, you, city, my, surely, very

Irregular pronunciation: **says, they**

Dictate the vocabulary words and some of the words with *y*. Students should exchange papers and grade each other's work as you write the words correctly on the board.

Spelling
5–8 minutes

Grammar Review

Ask the students to refer to the paper you gave them during the reading exercise. Ask them to find all the instances of the preposition *of* and tell how it is being used each time it appears:

Grammar
20 minutes

1. Who or what does it belong to?
2. What is it made from?

Answers:
On the first day **of** (usage 1) the Festival **of** (usage 2) Thin Bread, Jesus' disciples came to him and asked, "Where do you want us to prepare the Passover meal?"

(You could say, "the festival's first day," so usage 1 is correct. You could say, "the Thin Bread Festival," so usage 2 is correct.)

When Jesus was eating with his twelve disciples that evening, he said, "One **of** (usage 1) you will surely hand me over to my enemies."

("One" belongs to the group of "you," so usage 1 is correct. Usage 2 is not correct because "one" is not composed of, or made of, "you.")

He answered, "One **of** (usage 1) you men who has eaten with me from this dish will betray me. The Son **of** (usage 1) Man will die, as the Scriptures say."

(For the first *of*, see the explanation above. For the second *of*, usage 1 is correct because Jesus is calling himself "the Son" of "man," meaning all mankind, so he considers that he belongs to that group.)

The Preposition *To*

The word *to* is one of the most common English words. It has many uses, but today we are going to look at it as a preposition of movement or direction.

The Preposition *To* for Movement/Direction

Most of the time, *to* will appear after a verb and show movement or direction from that place to another. The first time it occurs in today's passage is in the first verse. Write this on the board:

- Jesus' disciples came **to** him and asked ...

Ask the students how *to* shows movement or direction in this phrase. (It shows that the disciples were somewhere else, then they arrived at the place where Jesus was.)

To As Part of an Infinitive Verb

Here's the next occurrence of *to*. Write the following verse on the board, and ask the students to describe how *to* is being used:

- "Where do you want us **to** prepare the Passover meal?"

This time, the word *to* is not being used as a preposition but as part of the infinitive of the base verb *prepare*. This time, *to* comes before the verb. There is no movement associated with this use. *Want* is the verb in this sentence, and the infinitive verb phrase *to prepare* is being used as a noun, answering the question "What do you want?"

Noticing whether *to* comes before the verb (infinitive) or after the verb (preposition) is the best way to know how *to* is being used in a sentence. If it comes between two verbs, the context of the sentence can help you determine how it is being used.

Continue in this way as long as you have time. Ask students to find the next example of the word *to* and write it on the board. Ask them if it is being used as a preposition of movement/direction or as part of a base form of the verb. Here are the rest of the examples:

- Jesus told them **to** (*comes before the verb "go" as part of the infinitive*) go **to** (*preposition of movement/direction*) a certain man in the city and tell him ...

- "I want **to** (*comes before the verb "eat" as part of the infinitive*) eat the Passover meal."

- "One of you will surely hand me over **to** (*preposition of movement/direction*) my enemies."

- Each one said **to** (*preposition of movement/direction—directing their speech at Jesus*) Jesus ...

- It's going **to** (*comes before the verb "be" as part of the future tense*) be terrible for the one who betrays me!

Don't Use *To* with This Common Verb

Tell the students that one verb of movement that cannot use *to* is *arrive*. With this verb, they have to use the preposition *at*—we arrive "at" a place, not "to" a place.

- "They **arrived at** Salamis and began to preach God's message in the synagogues." (Acts 13:5)

- "The evening before this man **arrived at** my house ..." (Ezekiel 33:22)

- "During the attack, Nebuchadnezzar himself **arrived at** the city." (2 Kings 24:11)

Write the following phrases on the board and ask students to think of a prepositional phrase using *to* that will finish the sentence.

Writing

10–15 minutes

- I am going ...
- She talked ...
- Marco and Luca went ...
- We're driving ...
- The grandparents arrived ... (Make sure they use *at*, not *to*.)

Have them write their sentences in their notebooks. When they are finished, put them into groups of two or three to share their sentences. Ask for volunteers to write one of their sentences on the board to share with the class.

The Story of Easter

Lesson 5

The Lord's Supper

During the meal Jesus took some bread in his hands. He blessed the bread and broke it. Then he gave it to his disciples and said, "Take this and eat it. This is my body."

Jesus picked up a cup of wine and gave thanks to God. He then gave it to his disciples and said, "Take this and drink it. This is my blood, and with it God makes his agreement with you. It will be poured out, so that many people will have their sins forgiven. From now on I am not going to drink any wine, until I drink new wine with you in my Father's kingdom." Then they sang a hymn and went out to the Mount of Olives. (Matthew 26:26–30)

Use any or all of the following introduction questions or write your own. Write them on the board so the students can read them as you ask them out loud, and refer to them while they compose their answers.

Introduce the Lesson
5–10 minutes

- What do you think Jesus was talking about when he said that God was making an agreement with his followers?
- Christians today still celebrate the Lord's Supper. Have you heard of this before? If you have, what does it mean to you?

Write the following comprehension questions on the board before you read the passage above so students have an idea of what they are about to hear and have specific information to listen for.

Listening Comprehension
10–15 minutes

- What did Jesus say the bread was? (his body)
- What did Jesus say the wine was? (his blood)
- Where did they go after they sang a hymn? (the Mount of Olives)

Read the verse to the students several times and ask them to answer the questions based on their listening.

Write the following words on the board and pronounce each one as you write the definition. If the word is a verb, conjugate it after you have worked through the meaning and pronunciation.

Say the word slowly with obvious stress on the accented syllable. Ask students if they can tell which syllable is stressed. Mark the syllable that gets stress and say it again. Write a sample verse or two, read it, and have the students repeat it.

1. during
(preposition)–all through a period of time
/ˈdʊr ɪŋ/

"My thoughts turn to you **during** the night." (Psalm 63:6)

"Its gates are always open **during** the day, and night never comes." (Revelation 21:25)

2. meal
(noun)–an occasion when people eat food together
/mɪəl/

"No one at the **meal** understood what Jesus meant." (John 13:28)

"A **meal** had been prepared for Jesus." (John 12:2)

3. blessed
(adjective)–holy, fortunate, or having a sense of peace or freedom from worry or pain
/blest/

"God **blessed** the seventh day and made it special." (Genesis 2:3)

"You have already **blessed** my family, and I know you will bless us forever." (1 Chronicles 17:27)

4. agreement
(noun)–an arrangement, promise, or contract made with somebody
/ə ˈgriː mənt/

"Our Lord, you are the friend of your worshipers, and you make an **agreement** with all of us." (Psalm 25:14)

"Then he said, 'This is my blood, which is poured out for many people, and with it God makes his **agreement**.'" (Mark 14:24)

5. forgiven
(adjective, from the verb forgive)–to not be blamed or punished for something you have done wrong

/fɚ ˈgɪv ən/

"If we truly love God, our sins will be **forgiven**." (Proverbs 16:6)

"Christ sacrificed his life's blood to set us free, which means our sins are now **forgiven**." (Ephesians 1:7–8)

Hand out the Bible passage written on paper and let the students read it. Read it out loud for the students as they read along silently to themselves. If they need you to read it again, do so. Ask if there are questions about any of the words.

Reading
5–10 minutes

Read the Bible passage a few words at a time, and have the students repeat the words out loud after you. Go slowly the first time, then again, then a couple of times at regular speed. Correct any pronunciation as necessary. Then try shadowing, where the students say the verse with you at the same time.

Speaking
5–7 minutes

Ask, "Do you think the disciples understood what Jesus was talking about?" Have a short discussion about the passage.

Pronunciation Review

Ask the students to refer again to the paper you gave them during the reading exercise. Ask them to find the letter *y*. Write the following words on the board, review the rules, practice the words, and check students' pronunciation.

Pronunciation
20 minutes

my, body, you, many, any, hymn

Linking Consonants to Vowels

To introduce the concept of word linking, ask students what they think of when they imagine a robot speaking. Maybe something like:

Hello. My. Name. Is. Siri.

Siri has come a long way, but students will likely remember how AI from just ten years ago spoke. We know that's not how people speak in any language. The way native speakers link words together can make listening difficult for language learners.

Tell your students that words in a sentence are linked together when we pronounce them. We often link the last sound and the first sound of consecutive words. Write the following on the board.

Consonant to Vowel

Say, "Today, we're going to talk about how words are linked together with consonants and vowels. This is the most frequent kind of word linking, and it is an important part of English pronunciation."

Consonant-to-vowel linking is all about the sound, which makes English spelling difficult. Because many English words end with consonants, native

If your students enjoy these conversational English pronunciation exercises, include them in your lessons more often.

For extra resources, try Rachel's English Videos on YouTube. Rachel has what she calls "Ben Franklin Exercises," which break various sentences down into the elements of their pronunciation in a similar way.[2]

speakers will often remove the ending consonant of one word and attach it to the beginning of the next word if that word begins with a vowel.

Write the following sentence on the board:

- Then they sang a hymn and went out to the Mount of Olives.

Say it for the students at normal speed with normal pronunciation and have them repeat. Remind them that it is the sound that is important, not the letter being used. (Example: the "ey" from "they" ends with a long *a* sound, even though the letter *y* is technically a consonant.) Ask if they notice where the words are linked together. Add the following marks to the sentence:

- Then they sang‿a hymn‿and went‿out to the Mount‿of‿Olives.

The sentence sounds more like this:

- Then thay sanga hymən wenou| tə th'MounuvOlivz.

Let students try to pronounce "MounuvOlivz" as one word. Stress will be on the nouns *Mount* and the first syllable of *O-lives*.

Notice that the final *d* of "and" and the *o* of "to" disappear when they are linked. The final *t* sounds of "went" and "Mount" will likely disappear as well if the words are spoken quickly. There will not even be a "stop" to the *t*.

Work on the rest of the combinations in this sentence:

- thaysanga
- hymən'
- wen'ou|tə—the symbol "|" indicates a stop "t"

Ask students to repeat the whole sentence with you, working to combine the words together. Repeat as necessary. Students might have some fun with this because it really doesn't make sense; it just is what it is.

Spelling
5–8 minutes

Dictate the vocabulary words to the students. The words should be somewhat familiar, as you have just studied them. Tell them you are going to say them only twice at normal speed, and they will need to listen carefully.

Students should exchange papers and grade each other's work as you write the words correctly on the board.

Grammar
20 minutes

Let's continue our discussion of prepositions by looking at prepositions of time. Three of these will be the same prepositions we looked at when we studied prepositions of location in lesson 2. The fourth is new and is used in our text today: *during*.

Four Prepositions of Time: *In, On, At,* and *During*

With prepositions of time, it isn't so much about definitions and rules as it is about common usage. However, we can break it down into four general rules. Write the following on the board:

In: for months, years, centuries, and periods of time
On: for days and dates
At: for a precise time
During: through a period of time

In

Let's go one by one through these prepositions. Write the following on the board:

in: years and months (in 2020, in December)
    decades and centuries (in the seventies, in the 1800s)
    seasons (in the winter)
    times of day (in the morning)

Ask students to notice two things about *in*:

1. We are talking about a time *period*, not a specific time. Our activity is contained "in" that time period. It could be anytime in December or anytime in 2020.

2. Unless you are talking about a specific month (December) or a specific year (2020), we typically add the article *the* or *a*: "in the evening," "in a little bit."

Here are some sample Scripture verses:

- "**In** the beginning God created the heavens and the earth." (Genesis 1:1)

- "One will be sacrificed **in** the morning, and the other **in** the evening." (Numbers 28:4)

- "John baptized with water, but **in** a few days you will be baptized with the Holy Spirit." (Acts 1:5)

On

Write the following on the board:

on: days (on Monday, on your birthday, on Christmas Day)
    dates (on September 3, on July 4th)
    days with time periods (on Monday morning)

Here are some sample Scripture verses and a sample sentence:

- "Why are your disciples picking grain **on** the Sabbath?" (Matthew 12:2)

- "Very early **on** Sunday morning the women went to the tomb." (Luke 24:1)

- I have a doctor's appointment **on** Tuesday, March 6th.

At

Write the following on the board:

> **at:** times of day told by the clock (at 8:00, at noon)
> holiday periods (at Christmas, at Easter)
> specific timeframes or events (at dinnertime, at lunch)
> various uses with no specific rule (at night, at dawn, at midnight)

At usually refers to a specific time, while *on* usually refers to a more general time. However, note for your students these common exceptions that just have to be memorized:

- We say "at night" and "at noon," but we say "in the morning," "in the afternoon," and "in the evening."
- We commonly say, "What time are you leaving?" not "At what time are you leaving?" The answer would be "I'm leaving **at** eight o'clock."

Here are some sample Scripture verses:

- "So Joseph died in Egypt **at** the age of 110." (Genesis 50:26)

- "I usually set a prisoner free for you **at** Passover." (John 18:39)

- "The ones who had been hired **at** five in the afternoon were given a full day's pay." (Matthew 20:9)

During

During is used with a noun and tells that something happened within a certain time period. Here are some sample Scripture verses:

- "Jesus said to his disciples, '**During** this very night, all of you will reject me.'" (Matthew 26:31)

- "**During** Passover the governor always freed a prisoner chosen by the people." (Matthew 27:15)

- "Give them the power to collect the grain **during** those good years." (Genesis 41:35)

Worksheet

Now that you have given an overview of these four prepositions of time, students can work independently or in groups on the worksheet in Appendix B. Give them a time limit depending on their ability, perhaps three to five minutes. Have them check their answers with each other in pairs or small groups. As a class, ask for volunteers to answer. Discuss wrong answers and provide the correct ones.

For more practice with prepositions of time, add prepositional phrases to the example sentence. Do a sample sentence together as a class. Write the following on the board:

> Writing
> 10–15 minutes

I go to class

Add some possible answers and ask students to suggest more possibilities. Here are some ideas:

- in one hour.
- on Fridays.
- at 5:00 p.m.
- during summer vacation.

Put students into pairs. Write the following phrases on the board and ask students to work together to decide how to finish each sentence using a preposition of time: *in, on, at,* or *during*. There are many possible ways to finish each sentence with different prepositions.

- We are going to visit my family
- Sarah has a day off
- Our plane leaves
- My daughter plays basketball

Ask for volunteers to write some of their sentences on the board to share with the class. Ask if you can make corrections. You might choose to save corrections until the end and review some frequent mistakes that were made by more than one student.

The Story of Easter

Peter's Promise

Jesus said to his disciples, "During this very night, all of you will reject me, as the Scriptures say, 'I will strike down the shepherd, and the sheep will be scattered.' But after I am raised to life, I will go ahead of you to Galilee."

Peter spoke up, "Even if all the others reject you, I never will!"

Jesus replied, "I promise you before a rooster crows tonight, you will say three times that you don't know me." But Peter said, "Even if I have to die with you, I will never say I don't know you."

All the others said the same thing. (Matthew 26:31–35)

Use any or all of the following introduction questions or write your own. Write them on the board so the students can read them as you ask them out loud and refer back to them while they compose their answers.

Introduce the Lesson
5–10 minutes

- Has someone ever broken a promise they made to you?
- Have you ever broken a promise you made to someone else? (Thought question—no need to answer out loud unless students want to.)
- Why is it important to think carefully before you make a promise to someone?

Write the following comprehension questions on the board before you read the Scripture passage so students have an idea of what they are about to hear and have specific information to listen for.

Listening Comprehension
10–15 minutes

- When did Jesus say the disciples would reject him? (During this very night, this night)
- Where did Jesus say he would go ahead of the disciples and meet them? (Galilee)
- How many times would Peter say he didn't know Jesus? (three)

Read the passage to the students several times and ask them to answer the questions based on their listening.

Write each vocabulary word on the board, and pronounce it as you write the definition. There are four verbs in this lesson, so after you have discussed the meaning, syllable stress, and pronunciation, ask students to help you conjugate the verbs in several of the verb tenses they are familiar with. Write one or both of the sample verses on the board, read them, and have students repeat.

1. reject
(verb)–to refuse to accept or agree with something
/rɪ ˈdʒɛkt/

Note: /ɛ/ is a more open pronunciation of the short *e* (/e/) sound. Both are found mostly in stressed syllables. /ɛ/ is typically used in American English. Look at the words *bet* (/bet/) and the name *Betty* (/ˈbɛ ti/). The difference is minor, so if your students pronounce either the open sound of *Betty* (with the mouth slightly open) or the more closed sound of *bet,* either works for English learners at this level.

"Our ancestors refused to obey Moses. They **rejected** him and wanted to go back to Egypt." (Acts 7:39)

"He will be **rejected** and killed, but three days later he will rise to life." (Mark 8:31)

2. strike down
(phrasal verb)–to deliver a blow and cause someone or something to fall
/straɪk daʊn/

"I will use my mighty power to perform all kinds of miracles and **strike down** the Egyptians." (Exodus 3:20)

"With your mighty arm, Lord, you will **strike down** all of your hateful enemies." (Psalm 21:8)

3. scatter
(verb)–to cause to move far apart in different directions
/ˈskæt̬ ɚ/

"He **scatters** frost like ashes on the ground." (Psalm 147:16)

"I **scattered** the people of Israel, but I will gather them again." (Jeremiah 31:10)

4. raise
(verb)–to lift something to a higher position
/reɪz/

"He **raised** his stick in the air and struck the rock two times." (Numbers 20:11)

"He **raised** me to my hands and knees." (Daniel 10:10)

5. ahead

(adverb)–in front, before

/ə ˈhɛd/

"Keep looking straight **ahead,** without turning aside." (Proverbs 4:25)

"I forget what is behind, and I struggle for what is **ahead.**" (Philippians 3:13)

Hand out the Scripture passage written on paper and let them read it. Read it out loud for the students as they read along quietly to themselves. If they need you to read it again, do so. Ask if there are questions about any of the words.

Reading
5–10 minutes

Read the passage a few words at a time, and have the students repeat the words out loud after you. Go slowly the first time, then again, then a couple of times at regular speed. Correct any pronunciation as necessary. Try shadowing, where the students say the verse with you at the same time.

Speaking
5–7 minutes

Talk about how someone can have good intentions, even make a promise as Peter did, but not be able to follow through. Why does that happen? Have a short discussion about the passage.

Voiced and Unvoiced *Th*

Th can make two sounds. The mouth position is the same for both, but the unvoiced *th* uses only breath (think, thistle), while the voiced *th* adds sound from the vocal cords (though, that).

Pronunciation
20 minutes

Many ESL students have a hard time pronouncing *th* correctly. It doesn't exist in some languages, but one or both of the sounds of *th* do exist in many languages and dialects, such as Castilian Spanish, modern Greek, Arabic, and some other Germanic languages.

Depending on the native language of your students, they may or may not have difficulty with this sound. If your students do have trouble, you might hear unvoiced *th* pronounced as an *s, t,* or *f* sound: *sink, tink,* or *fink* for *think.* Voiced *th* may be pronounced with a *v, d,* or *z—muhver, muhder,* or *muhzer* for mother. Here's a quick exercise to do with your students that should help.

How to Make the *Th* Sound Correctly

The only way to make the *th* sound correctly is to stick your tongue out a bit. The mouth is open, and the tip of the tongue touches the bottom of the front teeth, then drops down as the air is released. Try this exercise, being aware of any social mores or offensive gestures in the cultures you work with.

Ask the students to stick out their tongues. If they are reluctant to do this, remind them that they are learning a new language with new sounds. If they don't learn this common sound, their speech may not be understood well. Make sure all students, including you, are sticking out tongues, then set a timer for thirty

Teacher Tip

If your students are beginners, you might choose to focus on the voiced *th* instead of both sounds, as they need to learn the common word *the.* However, since the mouth positions are the same and the sounds are similar, students can probably learn both at the same time, even if they only practice one of them in this lesson.

seconds. Nobody speaks during this time, everyone keeps their tongues out, and you can occasionally point to a clock or your watch to assure students that you are keeping track of the time.

When thirty seconds are up, demonstrate the following words from today's Scripture passage and ask students to repeat after you. Demonstrate the distinction between the voiced and unvoiced sounds. Knowing whether the *th* in a word is voiced or unvoiced will be a matter of practice, as there are no rules. You may want to exaggerate the tongue motion of the *th*.

this, the, three, that, others, thing

Tongue Twisters with *Th*

If you are feeling brave, and your students seem like they would enjoy it, try a *th* tongue twister. Start slowly, then speed up a little as students are able.

- They thankfully think this thing is the best thing.
- There is my brother from another mother.

Optional Activity

Th is an important sound to learn, and students might have to concentrate to remember to say it correctly. Depending on your class, how well they all get along, and your students' ability to find humor in a situation, you could employ a mild "punishment" in the future for students who are habitual offenders of mispronouncing *th*. If you hear *s* or *t* or any sound other than *th,* ask the student to stick out his or her tongue for twenty seconds while the class continues. There is no need to have them repeat what they said incorrectly unless they ask what they did wrong. Just continue on with the lesson.

Dictate the vocabulary words and the *th* words you practiced to the students. The words should be somewhat familiar, as you have just studied them. Tell them you will say them twice at normal speed, and they need to listen carefully. Have students exchange papers and grade each other's work as you write the words correctly on the board.

Pronouns as Direct Objects

Let's look at a grammar topic that is handled differently in different languages. This lesson is an overview of pronouns as direct objects. We'll dig deeper into direct and indirect objects in a future series.

What Is a Direct Object?

A direct object is a person or thing directly affected by the action of a verb. Here are two examples:

- I am eating **an apple.** (noun)
- I am eating **it.** (pronoun)

Subject Pronouns vs. Object Pronouns

We are going to focus on using pronouns as direct objects. Quickly review pronouns with your students. Write the following on the board.

- Pronouns to use before a verb (subject pronouns):
    I, you, he, she, it, we, they

- Pronouns to use after a verb (object pronouns):
    me, you, him, her, it, us, them

Review these pronouns with your students and make sure they know the forms to use in the subject of a sentence and the forms to use in the object of a sentence.

Write the following sample sentences on the board and ask students to raise their hands and orally supply a subject or object pronoun that works with the grammar of the sentence.

- ___ are going to work now. (you, we, they—subject pronouns)
- We invited ___ to the party. (you, him, her, them—object pronouns)

Highlight the second sentence for your students. This sentence needs an object pronoun because the pronoun appears after the verb. This pronoun directly receives the action of the verb, so it is called a "direct object." If your students need more practice, take some time to do the worksheet in Appendix C, where students will choose the proper form of the pronoun for each sentence.

Direct Objects Come After the Verb

Emphasize to your students that in English, word order in a sentence is important. If words are not in the prescribed order, the sentence will be difficult to understand. In English, direct objects come after the verb.

Ask students to look at the paper with today's Scripture passage that you gave them during the reading exercise. Put them into pairs and ask them to find as many examples of object pronouns as direct objects (me, you, him, her, it, us, or them) as they can in three minutes. There are five. The answers are in bold type.

Answers:

- Jesus said to his disciples, "During this very night, all of you will reject **me**, as the Scriptures say, 'I will strike down the shepherd, and the sheep will be scattered.' But after I am raised to life, I will go ahead of you to Galilee."
- Peter said, "Even if all the others reject **you**, I never will!"
- Jesus replied, "I promise **you** before a rooster crows tonight, you will say three times that you don't know **me**."
- Peter said, "Even if I have to die with you, I will never say I don't know **you**." All the others said the same thing.

Teacher Tip

Your upper-beginner/ lower-intermediate students should try to become familiar with pronouns as direct objects before tackling the more complicated topic of pronouns as indirect objects.

Two of the pronouns could be tricky to find, because their sentences are compound and these direct objects are contained in a clause: don't know **me** / don't know **you**. Direct objects are always nouns or noun phrases following transitive verbs, and as such can be replaced by pronouns.

Review

Pronouns as direct objects can be confusing for your students in two ways:

1. They normally go *after* the verb. (In some languages, direct objects can go either before or after the verb.)
2. Object pronouns are different from subject pronouns.

More Practice with Pronouns as Direct Objects

Give the students a copy of the Bible passage from lesson 5. Put them in pairs and give them three minutes to look for all the pronouns that are used as direct objects. There are five; all are the pronoun *it*. Here are the answers:

- "During the meal Jesus took some bread in his hands. He blessed the bread and broke **it**. Then he gave **it** to his disciples and said, 'Take this and eat **it**. This is my body.'"

- "Jesus picked up a cup of wine and gave thanks to God. He then gave **it** to his disciples and said, 'Take this and drink **it**. This is my blood.'" (There are no more pronouns as direct objects in this passage.)

Point out again that all the direct objects appear after the verbs.

Writing
10–15 minutes

Dictate this verse from Luke 22 to the students. Read it three times, the first straight through while students listen. The second time, break it into phrases while they write. The third time, read it straight through while students proofread their writing. Pair students up again and let them compare what they wrote, then write the verse on the board so they can check their work.

When you come across punctuation marks, you can help students by saying, "comma," "period," "quotation mark," etc. You can also help them by writing any proper names, like "Simon," on the board to help with spelling. Here is the dictation text:

- "But Simon, I have prayed that your faith will be strong. And when you have come back to me, help the others." (Luke 22:32)

As time allows, have a discussion of how this verse relates to the passage from Matthew that we studied in today's lesson.

THE Story of Easter

Lesson 7

Jesus Prays

Jesus went with his disciples to a place called Gethsemane. When they got there, he told them, "Sit here while I go over there and pray."

Jesus took along Peter and the two brothers, James and John. He was very sad and troubled, and he said to them, "I am so sad that I feel as if I am dying. Stay here and keep awake with me."

Jesus walked on a little way. Then he knelt with his face to the ground and prayed, "My Father, if it is possible, don't make me suffer by drinking from this cup. But do what you want, and not what I want."

He came back and found his disciples sleeping. So he said to Peter, "Can't any of you stay awake with me for just one hour? Stay awake and pray that you won't be tested. You want to do what is right, but you are weak."

Again Jesus went to pray and said, "My Father, if there is no other way, and I must suffer, I will still do what you want."

Jesus came back and found them sleeping again. They simply could not keep their eyes open. He left them and prayed the same prayer once more.

Finally, Jesus returned to his disciples and said, "Are you still sleeping and resting? The time has come for the Son of Man to be handed over to sinners. Get up! Let's go. The one who will betray me is already here." (Matthew 26:36–46)

Use any or all of the following introduction questions or write your own. Write them on the board so the students can read them as you ask them out loud and refer back to them while they compose their answers.

Introduce the Lesson

5–10 minutes

- Do you have people you can call if you need help? If not, how could you find someone like that?

- Has a friend ever asked you for help? Briefly tell the class your story.
- Have you ever known the right thing to do but you couldn't, or didn't, do it?

Listening Comprehension

10–15 minutes

Write the following comprehension questions on the board before you read to the class so students have an idea of what they are about to hear and have specific information to listen for.

- What was Jesus going to do in the garden? (pray)
- Which three disciples did Jesus take with him? (Peter, James, and John)
- How many times did Jesus come back to find the disciples sleeping? (three)

Read the verse to the students several times and ask them to answer the questions based on their listening.

Vocabulary

10–15 minutes

Follow the same format you have used in the past when introducing new vocabulary words.

1. Write the word or phrase on the board.
2. Discuss the meaning.
3. Demonstrate pronunciation, including syllable stress.
4. Students repeat.
5. Write one or both of the sample sentences on the board so students can have an example of how it is used in a sentence.
6. Students repeat the sentence after you a few times.

1. take along
(phrasal verb)–to take someone or something with you when you are going somewhere
/**teɪk ə ˈlɑːŋ**/

"They **took along** every kind of animal, tame and wild, including the birds." (Genesis 7:14)

"Barnabas wanted to **take along** John, whose other name was Mark." (Acts 15:37)

2. troubled
(adjective)–having problems or difficulties
/ˈ**trʌ bəld**/

"We were **troubled** by enemies and **troubled** by fears." (2 Corinthians 7:5)

"Lot lived right and was greatly **troubled** by the terrible way those wicked people were living." (2 Peter 2:7–8)

3. go over

(phrasal verb)–to move from one place to another, especially when this means crossing something such as a room, street, or town

/gəʊ ˈəʊ vər/

"He told his servants, 'Stay here with the donkey, while my son and I **go over** there to worship. We will **come back**.'" (Genesis 22:5)

"Jesus **went over** to her and ordered the fever to go away." (Luke 4:39)

4. simply

(adverb)–emphasizes that something is easy or basic

/ˈsɪm pli/

"He will get up and give you as much as you need, **simply** because you are not ashamed to keep on asking." (Luke 11:8)

"There is only one God, and he accepts Gentiles as well as Jews, **simply** because of their faith." (Romans 3:30)

5. come back

(phrasal verb)–to return

/kʌm bæk/

"Jesus has been taken to heaven. But he will **come back** in the same way you have seen him go." (Acts 1:11)

"He told them goodbye and said, 'If God lets me, I will **come back**.'" (Acts 18:21)

Hand out the Scripture passage written on paper and let the students read it. Read it out loud for the students as they read along quietly to themselves. If they need you to read it again, do so. Ask if there are any questions about any of the words.

Reading 5–10 minutes

Ask, "If you were one of Jesus' disciples, how do you think you would feel if you couldn't stay awake as Jesus asked you to do?" Have a short discussion about the verse.

Speed Speaking

Here's a new speaking activity, "Speed Speaking," that many students enjoy. Ask them to remember a time they helped someone or someone helped them. While students are thinking, tell a personal story about yourself as an example. Ask them to stand and form two lines, with each student facing a partner. Tell them you are going to start a timer for one minute so they can tell their partners about a time they helped someone or someone helped them. When the timer goes off, the other partner will have a turn to speak for one minute.

Speaking 5–7 minutes

When the second one-minute timer goes off and both partners have had a chance to speak, one of the lines will take a step to the right so all students have a new speaking partner. Repeat as time allows or until each student has had a chance to talk to everyone in the opposite line.

Pronunciation

20 minutes

Unvoiced *S* and Voiced *Z*

The letter pair *s* and *z* is important for English students to learn because most plural words in English end with these sounds.

Make the *s* sound and ask your students to repeat. Then make the *z* sound and ask students to repeat. If they have difficulty, take some time to help them.

Explain that just like the two sounds of *th* that we studied in lesson 6, *s* and *z* have the same mouth position. The letter *s* is not voiced. The letter *z* adds sound from the vocal cords. Let them say *sss*, and while they are making the sound, add their vocal cords to make *zzz*. Ask them to hold their hands in front of their mouths when they say, "s." They should feel air coming out. Ask them to lightly touch their throats while they say, "z." They should feel their vocal cords vibrate. More air will come out of their mouths when they say, "s" than when they say, "z."

Minimal Pairs with *S* and *Z*

When the students are ready, write these word pairs (called "minimal pairs") on the board and demonstrate how to pronounce them. Have students repeat each pair after you.

> ice, eyes
> sip, zip
> once, ones
> bus, buzz
> close (adjective), close (verb)
> peace, peas

After students have repeated after you a few times, silently point to a word on the board and then point to a student, indicating that he or she should now say that word by himself or herself.

If your students are more advanced, ask them to notice that in these words, the *s* and *z* sounds are not always spelled with the letters *s* and *z*. It will take practice and repetition for students to learn the words and how they are spelled and pronounced.

If your students have trouble with these sounds, do a little more practice, then stop for today. If your students are able to pronounce *s* and *z* correctly, you can move on with an explanation of how to know when to pronounce each sound.

Teacher Tip

The following pairs of words are called "minimal pairs." Minimal pairs are extremely useful for teaching basic letter sounds. The pronunciation of both words in each pair will be identical, except for one sound—the sound you are focusing on.

Have students practice these minimal pairs exercises in a thoughtful and slow way, noticing how their mouths, tongues, jaws, and lip positions change as they say each word.

Knowing When to Pronounce *S* or *Z*

Distinguishing between the sounds of *s* and *z* is important for students to learn. Besides being used to form plural words, *s* is also added to the third person singular of verbs in the present tense.

Write the following words on the board:

sees, walls, feels, tables, chairs, cows, days

Pronounce them one at a time and ask students to repeat them after you. Ask the students what sound the *s* is making at the end of the word. (It's making the *z* sound.)

Write the following words on the board, pronounce them one by one for students, and have them repeat after you.

cats, eats, weeks, writes, maps, tickets

Ask the students what sound the *s* is making at the end of the word. (It's making the *s* sound.)

More Practice with *S* and *Z*

Ask, "When you see an *s* at the end of a word, how do you know which sound to make, *sss* or *zzz*?" They may not know. Explain to the students that there is a way to predict what sound the *s* will make so they will get it right almost every time.

If the sound preceding the *s* is a voiced sound (like the consonants *g, l,* or *r,* or any vowel sound like the *ow* of "cows" or the *ay* of "day"), the plural *s* will also have a voiced sound. It will say *zzz*.

If the sound preceding the *s* is an unvoiced sound (like the consonants *t, k,* and *p,* and the unvoiced digraph *th*), the s will also keep its unvoiced sound and say *sss*.

Let students suggest plural nouns as well as verbs that end in *s* and see for themselves that the rule works. Write them on the board so students can copy the words into their notebooks.

They may suggest words that are made plural with the -*es* spelling. Let them discover that if a word is made plural with an -*es*, it will *almost* always make the -*ez* sound.

churches, wishes, foxes, buzzes (all -*ez*)
knives (knivz)

Erase everything on the board. Dictate some of the plural words you just studied from the pronunciation section if they were mentioned and discussed—some with an *s* sound, some with a *z* sound, and some with an *ez* sound. Students should be able to spell them correctly. If you like, you can add the vocabulary words to the test as well.

Spelling
5–8 minutes

Tell students you are going to say the words twice at normal speed, and they will need to listen carefully. Have students exchange papers and grade each other's work as you write the words correctly on the board.

Introduction to the Verb *Get*

The verb *get* is a common workhorse verb with many meanings in English. It is the base verb for many phrasal verbs and expressions. *Get* is used twice in our text today. Let's take a closer look.

Conjugating and Pronouncing *Get*

See if students know how to correctly conjugate *get*.

- Present tense is *get* for most subjects and *gets* for third person singular
- Past tense is *got* for all subjects
- Present perfect is *have gotten* and *has gotten* (third person singular)

Conjugate other tenses if students ask. You may wish to note that *have/has gotten* is American English. British English is *have/has got*.

Get is relatively easy to pronounce, even though the pronunciation is irregular. *G* makes the hard *g* sound as in "gas." (It is irregular because typically when *g* is followed by *e*, it makes the softer *g* sound as in "gem.")

T is a stop consonant, meaning it is produced in two stages (see Teacher Tip). If the sound following the *t* is a consonant sound, as in "get down" or "get by," the air is not released to finish the *t* sound. If the sound following the *t* is a vowel sound, as in "get away" or "get in," the *t* becomes what is known as a "flap t." It is represented by /ɾ/ in the IPA. The tongue will tap the alveolar ridge behind the front teeth in a quick "flapping" motion, giving the *t* a slight voiced sound similar to *d* (/d/).

Review this pronunciation with your students until they feel relatively comfortable with it.

Get Meaning "To Arrive Somewhere"

Write the following verse from the Bible passage on the board:

- "When they **got there**, he told them, 'Sit here while I go over there and pray.'"

In this sentence, *get* means "to arrive somewhere." Write the following on the board:

get (to) + a place

This use is very common. People "get home," "get here," "get there," and "get to [somewhere]," like work, the store, the bus stop, etc. Write the following examples on the board:

Grammar

20 minutes

Teacher Tip

Stop consonants (*d, t, g, k, p,* and *b*) are made in two stages: first the air flow is completely stopped (with different parts of the mouth), then it is released to produce the sound.

For more information, check this article at Learn English with the Bible: https://www.learnenglish-withthebible.com/do-this-one-thing-to-help-you-sound-fluent/.

1. "Jonathan decided to **get to** the Philistine camp by going through the pass." (1 Samuel 14:4–5)

2. "When you **get to** Babylon, read this scroll aloud." (Jeremiah 51:61)

3. "When it **gets there** and finds the place clean and fixed up ..." (Luke 11:25)

Read each sentence twice to the students. The first time, say, "get to." The second time, substitute "arrive at" instead of "get to" for sentences 1 and 2. You may need to remind students that with the verb *arrive*, we need the preposition *at* (see lesson 4). For sentence 3, substitute "gets there" with "arrives there." *At* is not necessary in sentence 3 because there is no specific place mentioned.

In each of these verses, the word *get* has the meaning of "to arrive somewhere." Ask the students if they see how the meaning of "get to" is the same as "arrive at."

Let them suggest a few sentences of their own using "arrive at." Write them on the board and ask students to help you change "arrive at" to "get to."

Other Meanings of *Get*

Get has other meanings, but to list them all in one lesson would be very confusing. If you have beginners, stick with one meaning and one phrasal verb (we will look at phrasal verbs in the next sections). If your students are a little more advanced, and/or if they ask, here are two other common meanings of *get*:

1. to obtain, buy, or receive something (get + a direct object)

   - "**Get** some good lumber and build a boat." (Genesis 6:14)

   - "Peter replied, 'Remember, we have left everything to be your followers! What will we **get**?'" (Matthew 19:27)

2. to become, or to show a change (get + an adjective or comparative word)

   - "Abraham said, 'Please don't **get** angry, Lord.'" (Genesis 18:32)

   - "From now on, things will **get** better." (Haggai 2:15)

Using *get* in these ways is informal. See if students can think of a more formal verb that might substitute for the verb *get* in these verses. Here are some suggestions.

- **Obtain** some good lumber.
- What will we **receive**?
- Please don't **become** angry, Lord.
- Things will **improve**.

For most intermediate learners, these three meanings of *get* will be enough for the majority of what they will hear or read, aside from phrasal verbs with *get*, which we will look at next.

Get in Phrasal Verbs

Get appears in many phrasal verbs. It's easy to write a long list of phrasal verbs with *get* for your students, and they would probably like that. But for retention, it's best to learn and practice them one or two at a time. In this lesson, we'll look at three of the most common phrasal verbs with *get*. Your students may already know the first one.

1. **Get up**—to move from a sitting or lying position and stand on your feet

   - "**Get up**! Let's go. The one who will betray me is already here." (Matthew 26:46)

   - "Jesus took hold of the girl's hand and said, 'Child, **get up**!'" (Luke 8:54)

   - "**Get up** and go to Damascus." (Acts 22:10)

2. **Get into**—to enter a place

   - "At once, Jesus made his disciples **get into** the boat." (Mark 6:45)

   - "I promise you that you cannot **get into** God's kingdom, unless you accept it the way a child does." (Mark 10:15)

   - "It's easier for a camel to go through the eye of a needle than for a rich person to **get into** God's kingdom." (Luke 18:25)

3. **Get away**—to escape from a place or a situation

   - "Some Pharisees came to Jesus and said, 'You had better **get away** from here because Herod wants to kill you!'" (Luke 13:31)

   - "David and his men were on the other side, trying to **get away**." (1 Samuel 23:26)

   - "You won't **get away** alive, not even if you run fast or ride a horse." (Amos 2:15)

Let your students practice writing some of their own sentences with these three phrasal verbs. Share a few of their sentences with the class.

Get in Common Collocations

Many collocations with the verb *get* have the meaning of "to arrive," "to become," or "to obtain or receive." A collocation is not a phrasal verb; it's two or more words that are typically found together.

Make three columns on the board. Write the following definitions of *get*, one at the top of each column:

The Story of Easter

- arrive
- obtain/receive
- become

On the side of the board, write the following collocations, mixed up and without the headings:

Get (to become)
- get married
- get lost
- get hungry
- get sick

Get (to arrive)
- get home
- get [somewhere]
- get there

Get (to receive or obtain)
- get a call
- get permission
- get a job

Take a vote and ask students which category they think each expression belongs in. If the vote is not unanimous and correct, discuss with the class. Try substituting "become," "arrive," or "obtain/receive" into the expression to see which works best. When everyone agrees, write the expression on the board in the proper column.

Leave these collocations on the board for use in the writing exercise.

For practice with *get*, put your students into groups of two or three. Let them work together, choosing two of the collocations and writing a sentence for each one. Ask for a volunteer from each group to share their best sentence with the class. If the sentences are not correct in any way, point out where the problem is and ask the writers of the sentence if they can fix it themselves. Depending on how your class feels about being corrected by each other, you could ask other students to help fix the sentence before you supply the answer.

Teacher Tip

Collocation is a term used to describe a group of two or three words that are often seen together. They just "sound right" to native speakers. There are infinite examples, but common collocations include "fast food" and "round of applause."

Collocations are important for English learners because they can learn language in larger "chunks," which leads to more natural and fluent English.

Writing
10–15 minutes

The Story of Easter

Lesson 8

Jesus Is Arrested

Jesus was still speaking, when Judas the betrayer came up. He was one of the twelve disciples, and a large mob armed with swords and clubs was with him. They had been sent by the chief priests and the nation's leaders. Judas had told them ahead of time, "Arrest the man I greet with a kiss."

Judas walked right up to Jesus and said, "Hello, teacher." Then Judas kissed him.

Jesus replied, "My friend, do what you came for."

The men grabbed Jesus and arrested him. One of Jesus' followers pulled out a sword. He struck the servant of the high priest and cut off his ear.

But Jesus told him, "Put your sword away. Anyone who lives by fighting will die by fighting. Don't you know that I could ask my Father, and he would at once send me more than twelve armies of angels? But then, how could the words of the Scriptures come true, which say this must happen?"

Jesus said to the mob, "Why do you come with swords and clubs to arrest me like a criminal? Day after day I sat and taught in the temple, and you didn't arrest me. But all this happened, so that what the prophets wrote would come true."

All Jesus' disciples left him and ran away. (Matthew 26:47–56)

Use any or all of the following introduction questions or write your own. Write them on the board so the students can read them as you ask them out loud and refer back to them while they compose their answers.

Introduce the Lesson

5–10 minutes

- If you were in trouble, do you think your friends would help you? Do you believe God could help you?
- Do you think God knows what will happen in the future? How would believing that help you when you are in trouble?

Write the following comprehension questions on the board before you read to the class so students have an idea of what they are about to hear and have specific information to listen for.

- Who sent the mob to arrest Jesus? (the chief priests and the nation's leaders)
- What did Judas do after he greeted Jesus? (kissed him)
- Where did Jesus sit and teach day after day? (in the temple)

Read the Scripture passage to the students, once or several times if necessary, and ask for volunteers to answer the questions based on listening. Read slowly if you have beginners or if your students are more intermediate but need to improve their listening skills.

There is a mix of vocabulary in this lesson, including two phrasal verbs. These two phrasal verbs are relatively common, so you could work on conjugating them with your students. As usual, first explain the meaning of each word, then work on pronunciation, including syllable stress, and then use the word in a sentence for context.

Teacher Tip

Pull out and *put away* are transitive phrasal verbs. If a verb is transitive, it normally needs a direct object to receive the action of the verb. The direct object goes after the verb, and many times it can go between the two words if the verb is a phrasal verb.

put the coat **away**
put away the coat

pull the drawer **out**
pull out the drawer

However, if the direct object is a pronoun, it has to go between the two words:

put it **away** (never "put away it")
pull it **out** (never "pull out it")

1. mob
(noun)–a large, angry crowd
/**mɑːb**/

"That huge **mob** of Israelites will wipe out everything in sight." (Numbers 22:4)

"Jesus said to the **mob**, 'Why do you come with swords and clubs to arrest me like a criminal?'" (Mark 14:48)

2. greet
(verb)–to welcome someone, to wish someone well
/**griːt**/

"After they **greet** you, they'll give you two loaves of bread." (1 Samuel 10:4)

"**Greet** all of our friends who share in our faith." (Titus 3:15)

3. right
(adverb)–completely, all the way. Usually followed by "up."
/**raɪt**/

"You saw what the Lord did for you while you were in the desert, **right** up to the time you arrived here." (Deuteronomy 11:5)

"People were eating, drinking, and getting married **right** up to the day the flood came and Noah went into the big boat." (Matthew 24:38)

4. pull out

(phrasal verb)–to remove or withdraw something

/pʊl ˈaʊt/

"Go cast a line into the lake and **pull out** the first fish you hook." (Matthew 17:27)

"Jesus asked the people, 'If your son or ox falls into a well, wouldn't you **pull** him **out** at once?'" (Luke 14:5)

5. put away

(phrasal verb)–to place something in its designated spot

/pʊt ə ˈweɪ/

"My sword will never be **put away**." (Ezekiel 21:5)

"The Lord commanded the angel to **put** the sword **away**." (1 Chronicles 21:27)

Give each student a copy of today's Scripture passage. After they have read it quietly to themselves, read it out loud as they follow along. Ask if there are questions about any of the words, then read it out loud a second time.

Reading

5–10 minutes

Ask students to repeat after you as you read the first verse of the passage out loud again. Read at normal speed if you can, but if your students need you to read it more slowly, that's fine. It's better if they don't read the words from their papers because they may be confused by spelling and not pronounce the words correctly after you. You can read the sentences in chunks to help them remember what to say. However, if they are comfortable reading, let them read out loud after you.

Speaking

5–7 minutes

Repeat the first sentence two or three times. If your students are doing well, repeat with the second sentence. Continue as time allows. This is a long passage, so you don't have to do the entire thing.

For large-group discussion, ask, "What do you think Jesus meant when he said, 'Anyone who lives by fighting will die by fighting'?" Have a short discussion about the verse.

Pronunciation Review—*S* or *Z* Sounds

Before beginning the new lesson, review the pronunciation of plural words with *s* and *z* from the last lesson. Ask students to find the eight plural words in today's text. Don't say them out loud; just write them on the board as students pronounce them. Ask them why they chose to pronounce the final *s* the way they did.

Pronunciation

20 minutes

clubs (*z*–follows voiced *B*)

priests (*s*–follows unvoiced *T*)

leaders (*z*–follows voiced *R*)

lives (*z*–follows voiced *V*)

armies (*z*–follows voiced *E*)

angels (*z*–follows voiced *L*)

words (*z*–follows voiced *D*)

prophets (*s*–follows unvoiced *T*)

Making plural words can involve two or more consonants in a row, so make sure your students are pronouncing these clearly. For example, the *-rds* in "words" or the *-sts* in "priests" can be difficult for non-native speakers. Practice saying these words slowly, pronouncing each letter clearly.

Pronouncing *-ed* at the End of a Word

Another common English word ending is *-ed*. Write the following words from today's Scripture passage on the board, but don't pronounce them yet.

armed

replied

pulled

walked

grabbed

happened

kissed

arrested

Since you have just reviewed the rule about *s* and *z* making different sounds in different words, tell the students that *-ed* doesn't make the same sound in all of these words either. Ask them if they are familiar with pronouncing *-ed* at the end of a word. Many students will know that *-ed* is not always pronounced the same way in various words. If they are familiar with this concept, ask them to try to predict what sound *-ed* will make. Do this before you say the words for the students. If they are unsure, pronounce the words and ask students to repeat after you several times.

Ask, "Do you notice anything strange about how the *-ed* ending is pronounced?"

Answer: Sometimes it is pronounced as a *d*, sometimes it is pronounced as a *t*, and sometimes it is pronounced *ed*.

Ask, "How do you know which sound is correct to say?"

Answer:

- If the sound that comes before is voiced, *-ed* will also be voiced and be pronounced as a *d*.
- If the sound that comes before is unvoiced, *-ed* will also be unvoiced and be pronounced as a *t*.

- If the sound that comes before is a *t* or a *d*, then *-ed* will have its full pronunciation, *-ed*.

Pronounce the words on the board again and exaggerate the pronunciation so students can see that this rule holds true. Let them repeat each word after you several times.

Words That End in *-ed*

See if the students can tell you what kinds of English words end with *-ed*.

Answer:

- Regular verbs in the simple past tense end with *-ed*.
- Regular past participle forms also end with *-ed*.

Encourage the students to take out their copy of last week's Scripture passage. For the students who don't have it, pass out an extra copy. Put students into small groups of two or three, then ask them to find all the *-ed* words. When they tell you they are finished, ask a representative from each group to write a word on the board and use the rules to pronounce the word correctly.

Here are the words from last week and the sound each *-ed* makes:

troubled (*d*)
tested (*ed*)
walked (*t*)
returned (*d*)
prayed (*d*)
handed over (*ed*) (phrasal verb)

Dictate some of the *-ed* words you just studied from the pronunciation section. Students should be able to spell them correctly by putting an *-ed* on the end of each word, even though they are pronounced differently. If you like, you can add the vocabulary words to the test as well.

Tell students you are going to say the words twice at normal speed, and they will need to listen carefully. Have students exchange papers and grade each other's work as you write the words correctly on the board.

Spelling
5–8 minutes

Making and Pronouncing Possessives

We've looked at adding *-s* and *-es* to a word to make it plural. In our text today, we see words that have "apostrophe + *s*" to show possession.

Write the following on the board and pronounce for students:

- Moses' followers (Moses-*ez*)
- Jesus' disciples (Jesus-*ez*)
- nation's leaders (nation-*z*)
- Peter's friends (Peter-*z*)

Grammar
20 minutes

The first thing for students to notice is that "apostrophe + *s*" is used with normal nouns, like *nation's*, as well as proper nouns, like *Peter's*. Some students may have been taught that "apostrophe + *s*" is only used with proper nouns, but this is not correct.

Here's the second thing for students to notice. Write "Jesus's" (with the "apostrophe + *s*") on the board.

Ask, "Is there anything different about this spelling of *Jesus's*?"

Answer: When a word ends in *s*, we can make the possessive two ways: *Jesus'* or *Jesus's* with an extra *s*. Nowadays, either is correct, though current writing style guides suggest spelling it with the extra *s*: *Jesus's*. Since the CEV Bible uses *Jesus'*, I have chosen that spelling for this book.

Write the following on the board.

- the boys' shoes
- the dogs' food

Plural nouns usually end in *-s*. If three boys all have shoes, you would not say, "the boys's shoes." If you have three dogs and they all eat the same food, you would not say, "the dogs's food." We use just the apostrophe without an extra *s*. Context will help provide the correct meaning when you hear it spoken and can't see it written.

It's All About Pronunciation

Write the following on the board.

- the children's toys

Tell the students that sometimes you *do* need to use the "apostrophe + *s*" with plural words. The word *children* is an irregular plural. Since it does not end in *s*, we use "apostrophe + *s*" to form the possessive.

Children is probably a word your students have learned and use a lot, so it is helpful to know how to make this possessive. Other examples of making a plural word possessive with "apostrophe + *s*" are *men's*, *women's*, *people's*, and *mice's*.

For extra practice, repeat the pronunciation of everything you have written on the board. Saying the *s* + *z* sound of some words, like *Jesus-ez*, may be difficult.

More Examples

Here are some other phrases, some from the Bible, that show possession. Write them silently on the board and ask your students to practice pronouncing them. Make gentle corrections if necessary.

- "Moses, the Lord's servant" (Joshua 12:6)
- "The Lord's temple and Solomon's palace" (1 Kings 9:1)
- Michael's car

- The city's laws
- My brother's job
- Scott's apartment

The Lord's Servant vs. the Servant of the Lord

"Apostrophe + *s*" is not the only way we can show possession in English. This may be confusing to learners, because knowing the best way to make a word possessive depends on hearing it spoken repeatedly so it "sounds right" to say it that way.

Write the following on the board:

- The servant of the Lord
- The temple of the Lord
- The palace of Solomon
- The laws of the city

In lesson 3, we talked about how we can use the preposition *of* to show who or what something belongs to, though it isn't common in English. Tell the students they can sometimes use *of* to show possession, but it is more formal.

- When you say, "the laws of the city," the laws are more important than the city.
- When you say, "the city's laws," the city is more important than the laws.

When the owner of the thing is a person (either a proper name like Scott or a general noun like brother) or something animate (like a dog), we almost always use "apostrophe + *s*" because the owner of the thing is more important than the thing. *Michael's car* emphasizes that Michael is more important than the car. Generally, the word that comes first will be more important. We would not say:

- The car of Michael (We would say, "Michael's car")
- The job of my brother (We would say, "my brother's job")
- The apartment of Scott (We would say, "Scott's apartment")

Explain to the students that listening practice is important. Hearing the way things are commonly said is the best way to know how to form the possessive.

Do a dictation exercise to review the sounds of *s* and *-ed* as well as possessives. You can use all three of the following sentences or as many as you have time for.

Read each sentence three times. The first time, tell the students to leave their pencils on the table and just listen. Read it straight through at a normal speed. The second time, break it into short phrases as students write. Repeat each phrase twice, three times if asked. Speak slowly. You can say "comma" or "period" to indicate where the punctuation goes. However, don't mention where the apostrophes go. Read the sentence again so students can check their work.

Writing

10–15 minutes

- Mrs. Smith's apple pies tasted like my mother's pies.
- My sister's dog chased a rabbit into the neighbor's yard.
- Harold's family loved the library's selection of new books.

Ask for three volunteers to come up and write one of the three sentences on the board. Ask the rest of the class to help fix the sentences. Make sure all the corrections have been made and the sentence is correct.

Jesus Is Questioned by the Council

After Jesus had been arrested, he was led off to the house of Caiaphas the high priest. The nation's leaders and the teachers of the Law of Moses were meeting there. But Peter followed along at a distance and came to the courtyard of the high priest's palace. He went in and sat down with the guards to see what was going to happen.

The chief priests and the whole council wanted to put Jesus to death. So they tried to find some people who would tell lies about him in court. But they could not find any, even though many did come and tell lies. At last, two men came forward and said, "This man claimed he could tear down God's temple and build it again in three days."

The high priest stood up and asked Jesus, "Why don't you say something in your own defense? Don't you hear the charges they are making against you?" But Jesus did not answer. So the high priest said, "With the living God looking on, you must tell the truth. Are you the Messiah, the Son of God?"

"That is what you say!" Jesus answered. "But I tell all of you, 'Soon you will see the Son of Man sitting at the right side of God All-Powerful and coming on the clouds of heaven.'"

The high priest then tore his robe and said, "This man claims to be God! We don't need any more witnesses! You have heard what he said. What do you think?"

They answered, "He is guilty and deserves to die!" Then they spit in his face and hit him with their fists. Others slapped him and said, "You think you are the Messiah! So tell us who hit you!" (Matthew 26:57–68)

Use either or both of the following introduction questions or write your own. Write them on the board so the students can read them as you ask them out loud and refer back to them while they compose their answers.

- Why do you think that sometimes people don't want to believe what they see with their own eyes?
- Why do you think two people can see the same thing and have two very different opinions about it?

Vocabulary

10–15 minutes

Today we are going to do the vocabulary exercise before we do the listening exercise. Review the five vocabulary words as you usually do.

1. Write it and provide the meaning.
2. Pronounce it with syllable stress; students repeat.
3. Use it in a sample sentence or two.
4. If it is a verb, conjugate it in several tenses and include the past participle form.

Teacher Tip

If you find that your class likes to do vocabulary before they listen, you can reverse the order of the exercises in future lessons.

Don't dwell too much on other words, because they need to focus on these five words for the reading exercise.

1. courtyard
(noun)–an open space that is partly or completely surrounded by the walls of a building, usually in a large home or palace
/ˈkɔːrt jɑːrd/

"Moses had the curtains hung around the **courtyard**." (Exodus 40:33)

"We went through the east gate to the inner **courtyard**." (Ezekiel 40:32)

2. tear down
(phrasal verb)–to destroy something intentionally
/ter daʊn/

"I'm going to **tear down** your tower!" (Judges 8:9)

"I'll **tear down** my barns and build bigger ones." (Luke 12:18)

3. even though
(conjunction/idiom)–despite the fact that
/ˈiː vən ðoʊ/

"**Even though** what you did was wrong, you don't need to be afraid." (1 Samuel 12:20)

"God showed how much he loved us by having Christ die for us, **even though** we were sinful." (Romans 5:8)

4. at last

(expression, adverb phrase)–finally

/ət **læst**/

"**At last**, he reached Mount Sinai, the mountain of God." (1 Kings 19:8)

"**At last**, God sent his Son to bring his message to us." (Hebrews 1:2)

5. deserve

(verb)–to earn something (positive or negative) because of the way you have acted or behaved

/dɪ ˈ**zɝːv**/

"The Lord is great and **deserves** our greatest praise!" (Psalm 96:4)

"This man doesn't **deserve** to be put to death!" (Luke 23:15)

For today's listening comprehension exercise, make a copy of Appendix D for each student. This also counts as the reading exercise for today. As you read the passage out loud to the students, have them listen carefully for the vocabulary words and two other easy words and fill in the blanks when they hear the words spoken.

Read the passage a second time for students to check their work and fill in any words they missed. Pair them up to check their answers. Ask a volunteer to give you the answer for the first blank, then take a class vote to see who agrees or disagrees. Discuss until everyone agrees.

> **Listening Comprehension/ Reading**
> 15–25 minutes

Have a class discussion about the Scripture passage. Following are three more questions that might spark discussion. Feel free to create your own questions.

> **Speaking**
> 5–7 minutes

- What did Jesus mean when he said he would "tear down this temple and rebuild it in three days"?
- Do you know anyone who was punished for something they didn't do? Tell the class about it.
- What do you imagine Peter was thinking about when he sat down with the guards in the courtyard?

Pronunciation Review–The -*ed* Sound

Before beginning the new lesson, let's play a game to review the -*ed* ending from lesson 8.

> **Pronunciation**
> 20 minutes

Put students into small groups, being sure to distribute the more capable students evenly among the groups. Give them three minutes (or an appropriate time limit of your choosing) to find and write the seven -*ed* words from today's text. Groups should decide what sound the -*ed* makes in each word. If they remember from the listening, reading, and speaking sections, they will be one step ahead.

Ask the groups to stand when they finish. When the first group stands, stop the other groups from working as the first group gives you the pronunciations of *-ed* they found. If they are correct, congratulate them and see how the other groups did.

If the first group did not get all the words right, let the other groups continue in the same manner until one of the groups gets all the words right. The rest of the groups will have had the advantage of hearing what some of the correct answers are, and that will be a bonus for them as they work to quickly finish. You might want to make it a competition and have a small prize for the group who finishes first with all the correct answers.

Following are the words and their correct pronunciations.

followed (follow-*d*) (*d* follows voiced *o*)

wanted (want-*ed*) (*ed* follows *t*)

tried (tri-*d*) (*d* follows voiced *i*)

claimed (claim-*d*) (*d* follows voiced *m*)

asked (ask-*t*) (*t* follows unvoiced *k*)

answered (answer-*d*) (*d* follows voiced *r*)

slapped (slap-*t*) (*t* follows unvoiced *p*)

Pronunciation—More Consonant Clusters

As you say these words with *-ed*, you probably notice that adding the *t* or *d* sound after another consonant sound (like *claimed* and *asked*) can make the word more difficult to pronounce. Students may need extra practice saying these groups of consonants. Practice the seven review words with them, allowing them to start by saying the word slowly, then a little faster.

Today's text includes two plural words that end with the *sts* consonant cluster: *priests* and *fists*. The best way to pronounce the *sts* cluster is to not pronounce the *t* stop consonant completely. (This was introduced in lesson 7.)

With words like *priests* and *fists*, make the first *s* sound, then begin to make the *t* by raising your tongue to the area behind your front teeth to block the air and end the *s* sound. Instead of finishing the *t* sound, lower the tongue and make another *s* sound.

Pronounce these words for the students and let them repeat. You might want to use the "backward" technique to help you. Say the last letter of the word, then add the previous letters one by one until you can say the entire word.

- priests
  s–ts–sts–eests–reests–preests
- fists
  s–ts–sts–ists–fists
- asked
  t–kt–skt–askt

Try the same technique if there are any other words from the lesson that students are having trouble with.

You could ask them to repeat the following phrase from the Scripture passage. It is almost a tongue twister, so hopefully they will have a little fun with it. Write it on the board so they can read it and practice it several times.

- The high priest stood up and asked

Spelling
5–8 minutes

Dictate some words with consonant clusters that appeared in our Scripture passage today. The students may not remember these words, but let them do their best to spell them anyway. Pronounce them clearly but not in an exaggerated way.

fists, priests, courtyard, guards, temple, three, charge, witnesses

Tell students you are going to say the words twice at normal speed, and they need to listen carefully. Have students exchange papers and grade each other's work, then write the words correctly on the board.

The Word *About*

Grammar/ Writing
30–35 minutes

Let's return to our study of prepositions by looking at some meanings of the word *about*. We'll combine the grammar exercise with the writing exercise today.

Using *About* as a Preposition

About can be an adverb or a preposition. In this lesson, we saw it used as a preposition.

"They tried to find some people who would tell lies **about** him in court."

When *about* is used as a preposition, as it is in this sentence, it means "on the subject of" or "connected with." In this sentence, the lies would be "on the subject of" or "connected with" Jesus.

Following are more examples of the preposition *about*.

1. "He taught in their synagogues and preached the good news **about** God's Kingdom." (Matthew 9:35)

2. "The Lord answered, 'Martha, Martha! You are worried and upset **about** so many things.'" (Luke 10:41)

3. "I have heard **about** your faith in the Lord Jesus and your love for all God's people." (Ephesians 1:15)

As you write each of these samples on the board, ask the students what two things are connected with the word *about*.

Answers:

1. The "good news" on the subject of God's Kingdom
2. "So many things" connected with what Martha worried about
3. "Your faith" connected with what Paul had heard

About in Prepositional Phrases

As with all prepositional phrases, you will see *about* followed by a noun, a pronoun, or a noun phrase. Students will hear the preposition *about* often in phrases like the following.

- He talked about ...
- That book is about ...
- I'm thinking about ...

Writing Exercise

Write those sentence starters on the board. Working individually, students can choose one of the phrases and compose a sentence beginning with that phrase. (Examples: "I'm thinking about you" or "I'm thinking about what to make for dinner tomorrow.") Put students in pairs and let them compare sentences to check for correct grammar.

Ask for two or three volunteers to write their sentences on the board. Have the entire class help you check for good grammar and proper sentence structure. Ask them to notice what kind of word follows *about* when it is used as a preposition (a noun, pronoun, or noun phrase).

You can choose to stop the grammar lesson here since we've discussed the use of *about* as a preposition and done some writing practice. In the next section, I've included information on *about* used as an adverb if your students are ready for more.

Using *About* as an Adverb

About can also be used as an adverb, describing the action of a verb. When used as an adverb, the use of *about* can be different depending on the kind of English you are speaking. In this lesson, we are going to focus on American English.

When *about* is used as an adverb in American English, it refers to time and is a more formal way to say, "getting ready." It is followed by an infinitive verb with *to*. You can substitute the adverb *about* with the phrase *getting ready* in each of the following sentences.

- "What will be the sign that they are **about** to take place?" (Mark 13:4)

- "The Lord chose 72 other followers and sent them out two by two to every town and village where he was **about** to go." (Luke 10:1)

- "It was Friday, and the Sabbath was **about** to begin." (Luke 23:54)

Students will hear this in everyday phrases like "I am about to …" and "He is about to …." Ask the students to notice what verb comes before *about* in all of these examples (the verb *be*).

Writing Exercise

Write "I am about to …" and "He is about to …" on the board and repeat the previous exercise, asking students to compose one sentence beginning with one of those phrases. Pair them up to compare sentences, then volunteers can write their sentences on the board to check together as a class. After students have shared their sentences, let them substitute the more casual *getting ready* for *about* in their sentences.

Another Meaning of *About* as an Adverb

The adverb *about* can also mean "approximately" or "almost." It will come before (never after) a number or quantity when it is used in this way.

- "One day there were **about** 120 of the Lord's followers meeting together." (Acts 1:15)

- "**About** nine that morning, the man saw some other people standing in the market with nothing to do." (Matthew 20:3)

Writing Exercise

Repeat the writing exercise with the phrases "We had about …" and "Michael paid about …" In these sentences, *about* is a synonym with the word *around*. For example, you could say, "We had around …" or "Michael paid around …."

Following are some examples.

- We had **about** (around) one hundred people at church today.
- Michael paid **about** (around) fifty dollars for groceries today.

Two Common Phrasal Verbs with *About*

Two common phrasal verbs use the word *about* as a preposition: *talking about* and *worry about*. Students should practice these so they become familiar with them and understand easily what they mean when they hear them.

1. **Talk about**

Talk about is a phrasal verb that is used to emphasize the subject you want to discuss. When used this way, it will be followed by a noun, a pronoun, or a noun phrase.

- Let's not **talk about** that right now.
- They **were talking about** last week's storm.

It may also be used to indicate that either you or the person you are discussing understands what you are saying. In this use, it will not be followed by anything. Following are some examples of this use.

- "The man wanted to show that he knew what he was **talking about**." (Luke 10:29)

- "I am sure that King Agrippa knows what I am **talking about**." (Acts 26:26)

2. **Worry about**

Worry about is another phrasal verb that will usually be followed by the thing that concerns you. This will be a noun, a pronoun, or a noun phrase.

- "Jesus said to his disciples: I tell you not to **worry about** your life!" (Luke 12:22)

- "If we truly love others and live as Christ did in this world, we won't be **worried about** the day of judgement." (1 John 4:17)

- "Each day I am burdened down, **worrying about** all the churches." (2 Corinthians 11:28)

Writing Exercise

Repeat the writing exercise, asking students to compose one sentence with "talking about" and one sentence with "worry about."

Two Common Idioms with *About*

1. **How about …**

In American English, it is common to hear the idiom "How about …" This is basically a shortened version of "How do you feel about …" You are asking the listener what their opinion is. It's commonly pronounced "how 'bout" because the *a* in *about* is a schwa sound that disappears when words are spoken quickly.

- "**How about** some ice cream?" (How do you feel about having some ice cream?)

- "**How 'bout** those Yankees?" (How do you feel about those Yankees [the New York Yankees baseball team]? *The required answer is that they were, are, and always will be amazing.*)

2. **What about …**

"What about …" is another common American English idiom that means "What do you think about …?" It's commonly pronounced *wa-dabout*.

- "**What about** your brother Aaron, the Levite?" (Exodus 4:14)
  (What do you think about asking your brother Aaron?)

- **What about** that book you were reading?
  (What did you think about that book you were reading? Are you still reading it? Tell me about it.)

Many times, these two expressions are interchangeable. The meaning of the question is slightly different, but the answer can be the same.

- Where should we go shopping? **What about** the mall?
  Meaning: What do you think about going to the mall?
  Sample response: That's a great idea.

- Where should we go shopping? **How about** the mall?
  Meaning: How do you feel about going to the mall?
  Sample response: That's a great idea.

- **What about** taking a few days off (work)?
  Meaning: What do you think about taking a few days off?
  Sample response: That sounds like a good idea.

- **How about** taking a few days off?
  Meaning: How do you feel about taking a few days off?
  Sample response: That sounds like a good idea.

Practice with *What about* and *How about*
For practice with these two idioms, write the following on the board.

- What about
- How about

Ask for ideas to finish the questions. If students are unsure, ask them to think of an idea they could suggest to a friend for something to do after work or on the weekend. You could also suggest sentences like the following.

- What about Tom and Sally? Should we invite them?
- What about that new policy at work?
- You don't eat meat, do you? How about fish?
- How about going for a walk after dinner?

There are a lot of possibilities. Even just a pronoun will do.

- How about you?
- What about it?

Students probably won't learn these well enough to use them in their own speaking without a lot of listening practice, but they should be aware of the meaning if they hear these idioms spoken. The more students practice with these phrases, the more comfortable they will feel using them.

THE Story of Easter

Lesson 10

Peter Says He Doesn't Know Jesus

While Peter was sitting out in the courtyard, a servant girl came up to him and said, "You were with Jesus from Galilee."

But in front of everyone Peter said, "That isn't so! I don't know what you are talking about!"

When Peter had gone out to the gate, another servant girl saw him and said to some people there, "This man was with Jesus from Nazareth."

Again Peter denied it, and this time he swore, "I don't even know that man!"

A little while later some people standing there walked over to Peter and said, "We know you are one of them. We can tell it because you talk like someone from Galilee."

Peter began to curse and swear, "I don't know that man!"

Right then a rooster crowed, and Peter remembered that Jesus had said, "Before a rooster crows, you will say three times you don't know me." Then Peter went out and cried bitterly. (Matthew 26:69–75)

Use either or both of the following introduction questions or write your own. Write them on the board so the students can read them as you ask them out loud and refer back to them while they think of their answers.

Introduce the Lesson

5–10 minutes

- Have you ever formed an opinion of someone new based on what you know about their friends? Do you think that is a good way to judge a person or not?
- Can you tell where someone is from by their accent when speaking in your language? Is that easy for you or difficult?

Write the following comprehension questions on the board before you read to the class so students have an idea of what they are about to hear and have specific information to listen for.

- Where was Peter at the beginning of the story? (the courtyard, sitting in the courtyard)
- Peter talked like someone from what part of the country? (Galilee)
- What did Peter do after the rooster crowed? (he went out and cried bitterly, cried)

Read the Scripture passage to the students several times and ask them to answer the questions based on their listening.

Here are five new vocabulary words and expressions from this lesson. Feel free to substitute words that you think might be more important for your students to learn. Limit the words to five so students can remember them easily.

1. come up
(phrasal verb)–in this sentence, it means to move toward somebody or something
/kʌm ʌp/

"Dogs kept **coming up** to lick them." (Luke 16:21)

"He then invited Philip to **come up** and sit beside him." (Acts 8:31)

2. that isn't so
(expression)–you believe something is not true. If we make it a question ("Isn't that so?"), this means you believe something *is* true. You might want to spend some time with this and let the students think of sample conversations and sentences where they might use these expressions.
/ðæt̬ ˈɪzn ˈtsoʊ/

"'**That isn't so!**' Joseph insisted." (Genesis 42:12)

"In front of everyone Peter said, '**That isn't so!**'" (Matthew 26:70)

3. even
(adverb)–shows that something is surprising or unexpected
/ˈiː vən/

"Frogs were everywhere, **even** in the royal palace." (Psalm 105:30)

"God takes care of his own, **even** while they sleep." (Psalm 127:2)

4. a little while

(expression)–a short length of time

/ə ˈlɪʧ əl ˈwaɪl/

"Perhaps Onesimus was taken from you for **a little while** so you could have him back for good." (Philemon 1:15)

"My children, I will be with you for only **a little while** longer." (John 13:33)

5. bitterly

(adverb)–in a way that shows strong negative emotion, such as anger, disappointment, or regret

/ˈbɪʧ ɚ li/

"Today I complain **bitterly**." (Job 23:2)

"Many of the older priests ... wept **bitterly** because they remembered seeing the first temple years before." (Ezra 3:12)

In this lesson, let's combine reading and speaking by performing a roleplay.

Reading/ Speaking

10–17 minutes

Before asking students to read aloud in class, be aware of each student's situation and background. We usually do the reading exercise before the speaking exercise, because after students have heard and read the text, they will hopefully be familiar enough with it that speaking will not be a big issue. However, some of them may not be literate in their own language. They might be struggling with the Roman alphabet, or they may even have a learning disability. Roleplays can be a fun speaking activity, but keep these things in mind when asking them to read aloud individually in front of their classmates.

Students will "perform" this roleplay by speaking the separate parts. Choose a student for each of the six speaking parts: a narrator, Peter, Servant Girl 1, Servant Girl 2, Group Leader, and Jesus. Combine parts if your class is small. If your class is large, do the roleplay twice so all students can participate.

Copy the script from Appendix E and give one to each student. Let the ones who have speaking parts rehearse together for a few minutes while the rest of the class reads to themselves. Circulate and answer questions.

Groups perform their roleplay for the class. Don't correct pronunciation while students are speaking. Instead, choose a problem that seems common to most groups and go over it with the entire class after everyone has had at least one chance to speak.

Pronunciation Review—Consonant Clusters

Pronunciation

20 minutes

Let's start our pronunciation exercise by reviewing consonant clusters. This lesson has some good examples that you can review with your students. Remember that consonant clusters can appear between words too. Say the following phrases as students repeat.

isn't‿so
peopl‿standing‿there
and‿swear
rooster‿crowed
don't‿know

Remember from the last lesson that with "don't know" and "isn't so," the final *t* of the first word is a stop consonant—make the mouth position for *t*, stop the air, but don't release the air, just proceed to the next sound. We'll discuss stop consonants more in lesson 11.

Pronouncing *wh*

Not many words in English begin with *wh*, but the ones that do are used quite a bit. Write the following words on the board.

what

where

when

which

why

while (from today's vocabulary)

Tell students it is acceptable to pronounce this *wh* spelling as just *w*. Both the Cambridge[3] and Oxford[4] online dictionaries include this *w* pronunciation of the spelling *wh* for British English as well as American English.

wat

were (make sure it sounds different than the verb *were*—*wair* instead of *wer*)

wen

wich

wai

wile

Students may hear it pronounced with the *h* sound as a regional variation in some areas, such as parts of the northeastern United States. Practice this pronunciation if you think it would be useful for them depending on the kind of English spoken where they live.

hwat (what)

hwich (which)

hwear (where)

hwai (why)

hwen (when)

hwile (while)

Some words with *wh* are never pronounced with the *w* sound or the *hw* sound. They start with the *h* sound. Following are four common ones. Notice that the *wh* is followed by *o* in each word.

who (hu)
whom (hum)
whole (hol)
whose (huz)

Homophones with *wh*

Students may already know that there are many words in English that are pronounced the same way but are spelled differently and have different meanings. Below are some common *w/wh* homophones you can introduce to your class. Be sure students understand the meaning of these words, because the only way to know what word is being said is by understanding the context of the sentence.

weather / whether
wear / where
wail / whale
wails or Wales / whales
wine / whine

Dictate the vocabulary words as well as some words with *wh* from the pronunciation exercise. Be prepared to make up a quick sentence to provide context for the *wh* words that are homophones if you choose to use one of them.

Tell students you are going to say the words twice at normal speed, and they need to listen carefully. Have students exchange papers and grade each other's work, then write the words correctly on the board.

Spelling
5–8 minutes

The Word *While*

While is a good word to study, because it has many uses and meanings and can be confusing to students. Classifying the word *while* is difficult, and experts disagree as to what kind of word it is. It's not important that your intermediate students know what part of speech to call it; just help them understand the most common ways it is used in conversation. We'll do the writing exercise while we do the grammar exercise.

Grammar/ Writing
25–30 minutes

Using *While* as a Conjunction

The most common way to use the word *while* is as a conjunction that joins two clauses into one sentence. Today's text uses *while* as a conjunction with the meaning of "during the time that something else is happening."

- "**While** Peter was sitting out in the courtyard, a servant girl came up to him and said, 'You were with Jesus from Galilee.'"

Some sentences are "compound," meaning they are two separate clauses joined by a structure word like a conjunction.

A clause can be "independent"—capable of being a sentence by itself because it contains a subject and a verb.

A clause can also be "dependent"—it does not contain both a subject and a verb. It is not a complete thought by itself, and it has no meaning without the other clause or clauses in the sentence.

"While" is joining two independent clauses:

- Peter was sitting out in the courtyard.
- A servant girl came up to him and said, "You were with Jesus from Galilee."

During the time that Peter was sitting in the courtyard, the servant girl came up to him. *While* has the meaning of "during the time that something else was happening." In today's text, the two sentences have been combined into one sentence by using *while* as a conjunction, even though *while* is not placed between the two clauses. *While* usually appears at the beginning of a sentence, and the two clauses are almost always separated by a comma.

Examples for Classroom Practice

Example 1
Write the following independent clauses on the board.

- She was there.
- The angel of the Lord came to her.

Using the same construction as the first example, ask students to help you combine the sentences into one sentence that begins with the conjunction *while*.

Answer:

- "**While** she was there, the angel of the Lord came to her." (Genesis 16:7)

Example 2
Write the two independent clauses, then ask students to help you combine them.

- Jesus was still speaking.
- A crowd came up.

Answer:

- "While Jesus was still speaking, a crowd came up. (Luke 22:47)

Independent Writing Practice
Write "While I was at work," on the board. Ask your students to compose a sentence about something that happened at the same time they were at work. Feel free to change the phrase to better suit the situations your students are in.

After a minute or two, ask for a couple of volunteers to share their sentences by writing them on the board. Help them correct the sentences and make sure there is a comma between the two clauses if needed.

Using *While* as a Noun
While can also be used as a noun, and this use also appears in our text today.

- "**A little while** later some people standing there walked over to Peter."

While will almost always have the word *a* before it, indicating that it is being used as a noun. It means "a non-specific unit of time." It can appear with only the article, as in *a while*, or it may appear in phrases like *a little while*.

Students may also see it with words like *after, later,* or another reference to time. A comma may or may not be needed.

Below are some examples to write on the board. Ask students to point out all the articles (*a*) and the references to time (*later, for, longer, after*).

- "**A little while** later, the Lord told me to go back." (Jeremiah 28:12–13)

- "For **a while** the judge refused to do anything." (Luke 18:4)

- "Jesus told them, 'I will be with you **a little while** longer.'" (John 7:33)

- "Jesus told his disciples, 'For **a little while** you won't see me, but after **a while** you will see me.'" (John 16:16)

There are other meanings of *while*, but learning and practicing only one or two at a time will help your students remember and recall them more easily.

Independent Writing Practice

Write "After a while, we'll" on the board. Ask students to write a sentence that begins with this phrase. This time, pair them up and let them self-correct their sentences with their partners. After a few minutes, ask for volunteers to share their sentences either verbally or to come and write them on the board. Make gentle corrections.

The Story of Easter

Lesson 11

Jesus Is Taken to Pilate

Early the next morning all the chief priests and the nation's leaders met and decided that Jesus should be put to death. They tied him up and led him away to Pilate the governor.

Judas had betrayed Jesus, but when he learned that Jesus had been sentenced to death, he was sorry for what he had done. He returned the 30 silver coins to the chief priests and leaders and said, "I have sinned by betraying a man who has never done anything wrong."

"So what? That's your problem," they replied. Judas threw the money into the temple and then went out and hanged himself.

The chief priests picked up the money and said, "This money was paid to have a man killed. We can't put it in the temple treasury." Then they had a meeting and decided to buy a field that belonged to someone who made clay pots. They wanted to use it as a graveyard for foreigners. This is why people still call that place "Field of Blood."

So the words of the prophet Jeremiah came true, "They took the thirty silver coins, the price of a person among the people of Israel. They paid it for a potter's field, as the Lord had commanded me." (Matthew 27:1–10)

Ask the following questions to prepare students for what they will hear in today's lesson.

- Even if people are sorry for what they have done, is it fair that there are still consequences for their actions? Can you think of examples?
- Have you ever heard a news story about a person who was arrested for a crime he or she didn't commit? If so, how did it make you feel? If not, how do you imagine you would feel?

Introduce the Lesson

5–10 minutes

Write the following comprehension questions on the board before you read to the class so students have an idea of what they are about to hear and have specific information to listen for.

- How did Judas feel when he learned Jesus had been sentenced to death? (sorry, sorry for what he had done)
- What did Judas do after he had returned the money? (killed himself, hanged himself)
- Which Old Testament prophet predicted the purchase of the field with thirty silver coins? (Jeremiah)

Read the Scripture passage to the students several times and ask them to answer the questions based on their listening.

Today's set of five vocabulary words contains four phrasal verbs. Remind students that the first word is conjugated and the second word remains the same (tie up, tied up, will tie up, etc.).

1. tie up
(phrasal verb)–to make a person unable to move by putting a rope or something similar around the body. Also figurative—when a thing is unavailable for use because it is already being used.
/taɪ ʌp/

"We can **tie** him **up** so he can't get away." (Judges 16:5)

"He commanded some of his strongest soldiers to **tie up** the men and throw them into the flaming furnace." (Daniel 3:20)

2. lead away
(phrasal verb)–to guide someone or something where they don't want to go
/liːd ə ˈweɪ/

"**Tie** him **up** tight and **lead** him **away**." (Mark 14:44)

"Keep away from worthless and useless talk. It only **leads** people farther **away** from God." (2 Timothy 2:16)

3. pot
(noun)–a round container, normally used for cooking or holding plants. It may or may not have a lid. (You may wish to mention a few other kinds of containers used for shopping and cooking—pan, skillet, can, bag, package, sack, bottle, jar, etc.— and show pictures.)
/pɑːt/

"No one lights a lamp and puts it under a clay **pot**." (Matthew 5:15)

"I went there and saw the potter making clay **pots** on his pottery wheel."
(Jeremiah 18:3)

4. pick up
(phrasal verb)–to grasp something and lift it vertically (Another very common meaning is to remove clutter from a place.)
/pɪk ˈʌp/

"She asked if she could **pick up** grain left by the harvest workers." (Ruth 2:7)

"Jesus' disciples **picked up** twelve large baskets of leftover bread and fish."
(Mark 6:43)

5. belong to
(phrasal verb)–to be attached to someone or something by birth, dependency, or allegiance
/bɪ ˈlɑːŋ tə/

"Timothy, you **belong to** God, so keep away from all these evil things."
(1 Timothy 6:11)

"Anyone who **belongs to** God will listen to his message. But you refuse to listen, because you don't **belong to** God." (John 8:47)

Hand out the Scripture passage written on paper and let them read it. Read it out loud for the students as they read along quietly to themselves. If they need you to read it again, do so. Ask if there are questions about any of the words.

Reading
5–10 minutes

If students ask what *so what* means, you can tell them it means that your listener thinks that what you have been telling them is not important. It has a negative connotation and can make someone feel bad, so students shouldn't use it. You could talk about the situation in today's text where it is used by the Pharisees and how it was intended to make Judas feel helpless. Keep in mind the character of the Pharisee in the story who said it.

Ask, "Why do you think Judas felt sorry for what he did? Do you feel sorry for him too?" Have a short discussion about the verse.

In lesson 7, we introduced "Speed Speaking," where the students stood in two lines and talked briefly with each member of the other line. Let's use that activity to practice the four phrasal verbs from the vocabulary exercise today.

Speaking
5–7 minutes

Write any or all of the following questions on the board for students to ask and answer with their partners. You could also write them on paper and give a copy to each student. The first person in each pair can speak for one minute, then when you ring a buzzer, the other person speaks for one minute. Ring the buzzer again as a signal that they need to change partners. They can talk about as many questions as they have time for.

1. Does anyone you know have a dog? Do they tie it up outside, or does it live in the house?

2. Have you ever been late to work because you were tied up in traffic?

3. Have you ever seen a horse led away by its owner—maybe at a horse race or a county fair?

4. Besides empty talk, are there other things that can lead people away from God?

5. Do you have children? Do they pick up their rooms when you ask them to?

6. Have you ever asked someone to pick up a few groceries for you?

7. Do you know who that (choose something in view in your classroom: notebook, coat, backpack, etc.) belongs to?

8. Do you belong to a local church?

Pronunciation

20 minutes

Pronunciation Review

Keep students in the pairs they ended with in the speaking exercise. Let them return to their seats and ask them to work with their partners to find all the words in today's text that end with -ed. Ask them to decide how the -ed should be pronounced (as a d, a t, or an ed).

As a class, go through the words one at a time and ask one student how he or she decided to pronounce the word. Ask the rest of the class if they agree or disagree. If there is disagreement, discuss and ask why they chose to pronounce the -ed in that way. Here are the answers.

decided (decid-*ed*) (*ed* follows *d*—appears twice)

tied (ti-*d*) (*d* follows voiced *i*)

betrayed (betray-*d*) (*d* follows voiced *ay*)

learned (learn-*d*) (*d* follows voiced *n*)

sentenced (sentence-*t*) (*t* follows unvoiced *s*)

returned (return-*d*) (*d* follows voiced *n*)

sinned (sinn-*d*) (*d* follows voiced *n*)

replied (repli-*d*) (*d* follows voiced *i*)

hanged (hang-*d*) (*d* follows voiced *ng*)

picked (pick-*t*) (*t* follows unvoiced *k*)

killed (kill-*d*) (*d* follows voiced *l*)

belonged (belong-*d*) (*d* follows voiced *ng*)

wanted (want-*ed*) (*ed* follows *t*)

commanded (command-*ed*) (*ed* follows *d*)

Linking Consonant to Consonant

Linking words together will happen naturally over time with practice. Your lower-intermediate students may still have difficulty listening to spoken English if it seems to them that all the words run together. Examining how this happens will give them more confidence as they listen and speak. In this lesson, we'll discuss three ways consonant sounds are linked to other consonant sounds.

1. Linking Two of the Same Consonant Sounds

The easiest way to link consonants is to combine two similar consonant sounds. Look at this example from today's verses.

- Jesus should be put to death.

The name Jesus ends with an *s*, and the word *should* begins with an *sh*. We don't pronounce the *s* twice, with a pause in the middle. We only say it once, perhaps holding out the sound a little longer than normal: "Jesu(s-s)hould."

You also see the words *put to*. In the same way, we don't pronounce the *t* twice with a pause in the middle. We just say the sound once—pu(t-t)o. Practice these examples with your students.

2. Linking Two Different Consonant Sounds

Since many English words end with consonants, this way of linking is very common. Look at the following example from today's verses.

- nation's leaders met

Make sure students can pronounce each sound individually: *nz, nz, nz, l, l, l.* Ask them to pay close attention to their mouth position as they say each letter.

They should notice what parts of their mouths change position and what parts stay the same. For example, with *z* and *l*, their lips and tongues will move, but their teeth will stay mostly the same. Demonstrate the sounds, slowly at first, then a little faster. If students do well, try saying the combination at normal speed. Repeat with *z* and *m*.

Linking with *H*

Say the following word pairs for the students and ask if they notice anything different about the pronunciation.

- Lord had, tied him

Typically, when the second word starts with the letter *h*, the *h* sound is not pronounced at all: *Lor-dad, tie-dim.* Have students repeat after you.

3. Linking a Stop Consonant with Another Consonant

Stop consonants are letters that are pronounced in two steps. First you stop the air, then you release the air. There are six stop consonants in English: *b, p, t, d, g,* and *k.* The difference between the sounds depends on what part of your mouth you use to stop the air. The letters *p, t,* and *k* are voiceless; *b, d,* and *g* are voiced.

When a word ends with a stop consonant and the next word begins with a consonant, English speakers usually don't release the air of the stop consonant. They just move quickly into the next sound. This happens most often with *t* and *d,* but other stop consonants can do this as well. Demonstrate these examples from today's text for the students in an exaggerated way and have them repeat.

> but| when
> paid| to
> had| been
> took| the

This process of incompletely pronouncing a stop consonant is common in English. Below are a few more examples from today's text. Practice with the students.

> and| the
> decided| that
> learned| that
> returned| the
> can't| put (You may want to compare this with the pronunciation of *can put* so students can see the difference. It is not always easy to tell without some kind of gesture included.)

Ask students to read today's Scripture passage again, out loud together with you. Read slowly, asking them to take special care to notice where consonant linking happens.

Spelling

5–8 minutes

Ask the students to put away their copy of today's text. Replace it with the copy in Appendix F. Ten words in this worksheet are misspelled. Give students a time limit to circle the incorrectly spelled words, perhaps three to five minutes depending on their ability.

Pair them up to check their answers, then discuss the answers together as a class. If your students are somewhat competitive, you can see which student had the most correct, the second most, etc.

Grammar

20 minutes

Prepositions *By* and *With*

By and *with* are used to say how something happened. They connect "what happened" with "who or what performed the action." Let's start with the preposition *by.*

By Used as a Preposition

Write the following verse from today's Scripture passage on the board.

- "I have sinned **by** betraying a man who has never done anything wrong."

The verse says that Judas sinned. Ask the students to repeat the part of the sentence that says Judas sinned. (I have sinned). Now ask them *how* Judas sinned. (By betraying a man.)

The preposition *by* tells us how Judas sinned. Judas could have said either of the following.

- I have sinned.
- I have betrayed a man.

These two actions are connected because they are combined into one sentence with the preposition *by*.

- "I have sinned **by** betraying a man."

Write the following examples on the board and ask the questions.

- "I told myself, 'I'll be careful not to sin **by** what I say.'" (Psalm 39:1) How would he sin? (By what he says.)

- "You can tell who the false prophets are **by** their deeds." (Matthew 7:20) How can you tell who the false prophets are? (By their deeds.)

- "Was he like tall grass blown about **by** the wind?" (Matthew 11:7) How was the tall grass blown about? (By the wind.)

When *by* is used as a preposition, it answers the question of "how something happened." In a prepositional phrase, it will be followed by a noun, a pronoun, or a noun phrase.

The Preposition *With*

The preposition *with* has many meanings, but a good definition for your students is "people or things are in a place together or are doing something together." They probably have a corresponding preposition in their own language that will help them understand. *By* shows how something happened or who performed the action. *With* shows the connection between things without necessarily including an action, though it can.

Write the following verse on the board and ask your students to tell what things are being connected using the preposition *with*. Do the example verse together as a class.

- "The Lord said, 'I will go **with** you and give you peace.'" (Exodus 33:14)

Teacher Tip

By can also be used as an adverb, an adjective, a noun, and an interjection. When *by* is used as a preposition, it answers the question "how?" In a prepositional phrase it will be followed by a noun, a pronoun, or a noun phrase.

Teacher Tip

With is only used as a preposition. It has many meanings in the dictionary. However, the general idea of *with* is to connect two things. Students shouldn't have too much trouble with this, as it can probably be directly translated into their own language.

Like other prepositions, *with* will begin a prepositional phrase followed by a noun, a pronoun, or a noun phrase.

The students should tell you that *I* and *you* are connected by the preposition *with*. Now try the following. What two things are being connected?

- "The next morning the officials sent some police **with** orders for the jailer to let Paul and Silas go." (Acts 16:35)
  What were the police sent with? (They were sent **with** orders.)

- "Elijah and Moses appeared and were talking **with** Jesus." (Mark 9:4)
  Who were Elijah and Moses talking with? (They were talking **with** Jesus.)

- "The man answered, 'She is the one who came back from Moab **with** Naomi.'" (Ruth 2:6)
  Did she come back alone? (No, she was **with** Naomi.)

Writing

10–15 minutes

Write the following phrases on the board. Put students into pairs or small groups and ask them to finish the sentences. Give them a set amount of time, maybe five minutes, then ask for volunteers to share their group's best sentence by writing it on the board. Gently correct as necessary.

- I work with
- My children go to school with
- Jesus prayed to his Father with
- The dog asked me to play with him by
- We were surprised by
- I can tell you are happy by

The Story of Easter

Lesson 12

Pilate Questions Jesus

Jesus was brought before Pilate the governor, who asked him, "Are you the king of the Jews?"

"Those are your words!" Jesus answered. And when the chief priests and leaders brought their charges against him, he did not say a thing.

Pilate asked him, "Don't you hear what crimes they say you have done?" But Jesus did not say anything, and the governor was greatly amazed. (Matthew 27:11–14)

The Bible passage for this lesson is not very long, so you may have time to engage your students with more conversation. This is great speaking practice. Encourage all students to share if they like. Ask them the following questions:

Introduce the Lesson

5–10 minutes

- Have you ever met anybody famous? Have you seen a famous actor or musician at a live performance, or have you been to a political rally with a well-known politician? What was it like?
- Have you ever refused to "go along with" everyone else (to do what everyone else is doing) because you wanted to do the right thing? Was it difficult or easy?

Write the following comprehension questions on the board before you read to the class so students have an idea of what they are about to hear and have specific information to listen for.

Listening Comprehension

10–15 minutes

- What did Jesus say when Pilate asked him if he was the king of the Jews? ("Those are your words.")
- What did Jesus say to the charges of the chief priests and leaders? (nothing, he did not say a thing)
- How did Pilate react to Jesus' silence? (he was amazed, greatly amazed)

Read the verse to the students several times and ask them to answer the questions based on their listening.

The vocabulary words and expressions for this lesson are various parts of speech, so help students understand how they are used as you share the sample sentences. We will talk more about the preposition *against* in today's grammar exercise.

1. bring
(verb)–to come with somebody or something, to give or provide
/**brɪŋ**/

"He asked, 'Would you also please **bring** me a piece of bread?'" (1 Kings 17:11)

"I love your commands! They **bring** me happiness." (Psalm 119:47)

2. charge
(noun)–an official claim made by authorities that someone has broken the law
/ˈ**tʃɑːrdʒ**/

"Israel, I am your God. Listen to my **charges** against you." (Psalm 50:7)

"The chief priests brought many **charges** against Jesus." (Mark 15:3)

3. against
(preposition)–opposing or disagreeing with somebody or something
/ə ˈ**genst**/

"My friend turned **against** me and broke his promise." (Psalm 55:20)

"They insulted Paul and spoke **against** everything he said." (Acts 13:45)

4. a thing
(expression)–anything (used for emphasis)
/ə ˈ**θɪŋ**/

"Those people who disagree are proud of themselves, but they don't really know **a thing**." (1 Timothy 6:4)

"If our bodies were only an eye, we couldn't hear **a thing**. And if they were only an ear, we couldn't smell **a thing**." (1 Corinthians 12:17)

5. amazed
(adjective)–very surprised
/ə ˈ**meɪzd**/

"The officials were **amazed** to see how brave Peter and John were." (Acts 4:13)

"When the governor saw what had happened, he was **amazed** at this teaching about the Lord. So he put his faith in the Lord." (Acts 13:12)

Hand out the Scripture passage written on paper, and let students read it quietly to themselves. Ask if there are any questions about anything they are reading. Read it out loud for the students at normal reading speed as they read along quietly. If they need you to read it again, do so.

Reading

5–10 minutes

Put students into pairs or small groups. Write the following question on the board (or a question of your own choosing).

Speaking

5–7 minutes

- Why do you think Jesus didn't answer Pilate's questions?

Let students talk together for two to three minutes and monitor groups to make sure everyone is getting a chance to speak.

When you do a speaking exercise like this, don't correct students' grammar mistakes unless they ask you to. The purpose of this exercise is to help them feel comfortable and more confident when they speak in English. If they are making themselves understood, they are communicating well.

This may be a difficult question, so you could come back together as a large group and continue the discussion. You may also make up a question of your own for them to discuss instead of this one.

Pronunciation Review
Linking Consonants to Vowels
Linking Consonants Together

Pronunciation

20 minutes

Review with your students how to link a consonant sound to a vowel sound and how to link two consonant sounds together. Below are some examples from today's text. Write them on the board and let students decide ways they might be linked together, then practice pronouncing them.

- Those are
- Pilate asked
- Jesus was brought before
- Say you

Answers:
Consonant to vowel:

- those‿are (thozar)
- Pilat‿asked (*t* changes to "flap t" sound)

Consonant to consonant:

- Jesus‿waz‿brought| before ("stop t" before consonant *b*)
- say‿you (two letters make one sound)

Linking Vowel to Vowel

Today we'll talk about how to link two vowel sounds together. Please make sure this information is relevant to the English accent you and your students use.

In English, we don't often see a word that ends with a vowel followed by a word that starts with a vowel. However, even though the letters *y* and *w* are classified as consonants, they make voiced sounds that are similar to vowel sounds: *ee* or *ee-uh* for *y*, and *oo* or *oo-uh* for *w*. This is important to remember for two reasons:

1. Many English words end with *y* and *w*.
2. These two sounds serve as "buffers" between actual vowels, even if the letter *y* or *w* is not present in the word. This happens because it makes pronunciation easier. Let's take a closer look.

Linking Long *A*, Long *E*, and Long *I*

Ask students to pronounce these long vowel sounds after you: *a*, *e*, and *i*. Exaggerate the pronunciation with your mouth wide.

1. Ask them what position their lips are in as they say the sounds. (wide)
2. Ask them to say, "happy." What is the position of their lips when they say the *ee* sound at the end of *happy*? (wide)
3. How is this sound spelled? (*y*)

Write the following examples on the board.

- Way out
- We are
- Greatly amazed

If the first word ends with a long *a*, *e*, or *i* sound, and the next word begins with a vowel, very often English speakers will insert a *y* sound to blend the two vowels together. That *yuh* sound helps make a smooth connection between the words, because all the sounds are pronounced with the mouth wide.

Pronounce them for the class.

- Way out—waee + y + owt
- We are—wee + y + are
- Greatly amazed—greatlee + y + amazed

In two of these examples, the *y* is actually present in the word, even though it is making the long *e* sound.

Write the following sample sentences on the board, discuss how they are pronounced, and have students repeat after you. Emphasize the *yuh* sound that links the vowels together.

- He ate the apple.
  Hee + y + ate thee + y + apple.

- Mindy arrived very early.
  Mindee + y + arrived veree + y + early.

- They asked for the umbrella.
  Thaee + y + asked for thee + y + umbrella.

Linking Long *O* and Long *U*

If the first word ends in a long *o* or long *u* sound, your mouth is in a different shape. These sounds are made with your lips more narrow and rounded. Ask the students to pronounce these words, paying attention to the position of their lips:

- Who
- Yellow
- Knew

When the long vowel at the end of a word is *o* or *u*, the connecting sound is *w*. *W* has a similar mouth position to *o* and *u*. The *yuh* connecting sound doesn't work, because the mouth position is too different. Instead, the connecting sound is *wuh*. Look at the following examples.

- Who asked—whoo + w + asked
- Yellow apples—yello-oo + w + apples
- Knew you—kne-oo + w + you

Again, you can see that the first word sometimes ends with the letter *w*. Below are some sentences to practice with. Pronounce for your students and have them repeat, slowly at first, then normal speed.

- Babies grow up too fast.
  Babies grow + w + up too fast.

- You eat out too often.
  You + w + eat out too + w + often.

- Who asked you to open the door?
  Who + w + asked you to + w + open the door?

Don't Stress

Don't stress too much about this. After a little bit of practice, students will see that these extra sounds, *y* and *w*, are very natural. They won't have to think much about it, because these extra sounds make sentences more fluid and easier to pronounce.

Short and Long Vowel Sounds

In all of our examples, the first word ends with a long vowel sound, but the second word can begin with either a long vowel sound or a short vowel sound. Remember, the words don't have to end or begin with a vowel letter. It's the sound that is important.

- High up—high + y + up
  The *gh* is silent, so the word ends with a long *i* sound.

- Throw up—throw + w + up (to vomit)
  The *ow* makes the long *o* sound.

If a word ends with a short vowel sound, we don't use a *y* or *w* sound to connect them because the mouth position is different. It's not common for an English word to end with a short vowel, but it happens sometimes. Just move from one word to the other, pronouncing the letters completely. Below are some examples.

- Carla exited the train.
- Africa is a continent.
- I saw it.

Spelling

5–8 minutes

Dictate the five vocabulary words for students to write. Tell them you are going to say the words twice at normal speed, and they need to listen carefully.

They can earn five extra points by writing a sentence using the vocabulary word, for a total of ten possible points. Students should exchange papers and grade each other's work as you write the words correctly on the board. Ask for volunteers to share their sentences for correction.

Grammar

20 minutes

The Preposition *Against*

We'll cover two grammar topics today, since we have a new preposition in our lesson: *against*. If one topic is enough for your class, feel free to stop after we discuss *against*.

Opposing or Disagreeing

Against has several meanings, but in today's text it means "opposing or disagreeing with someone or something." The prepositional phrase beginning with *against* will tell who or what is being opposed. The subject of the sentence will tell who or what is doing the opposing.

Write this sentence from our text on the board. Underline "against him" and explain that this is the prepositional phrase beginning with the preposition *against*.

- "The chief priests and leaders brought their charges **against him**."

1. Ask the students who or what is being opposed? (him, Jesus)
2. Ask students to help you locate the subject of this sentence.
   (the chief priests and leaders)

To help students find the subject, you can circle the verb (*brought*) and remind them that the subject of a sentence comes before the verb.

Ask the students who is doing the opposing? Who is against Jesus? (the subject: *chief priests and leaders*)

Below are some more examples of this meaning.

1. "They insulted Paul and spoke **against** everything he said." (Acts 13:45)

2. "When we left Sidon, the winds were blowing **against** us." (Acts 27:4)

3. "I obey you completely and guard **against** sin." (Psalm 18:23)

For each of these examples, ask students to describe who or what is being opposed or disagreed with. They will find this in the prepositional phrase that begins with "against." Second, they should look at the subject to discover who is doing the opposing or disagreeing in each of these verses.

Answers:

1. Against who or what: everything he said
   Who is opposing or disagreeing? (they, the Jewish people)

2. Against who or what: us
   What is opposing or disagreeing? (the wind)

3. Against who or what: sin
   Who is opposing or disagreeing? (I)

You will find a worksheet with more of these questions in Appendix G.

Don't at the Beginning of a Question

Here is the second topic for our grammar lesson today. Use it if you have time or if you need to keep your more advanced students busy while your beginners finish the worksheet from Appendix G.

Your intermediate students have probably learned that in English, a negative sentence and a question both need the helping verb *do*. For a review, write the following sentence on the board and ask students to help you make it negative, then turn it into a question. Write all the sentences on the board.

- You have a bicycle. (sentence)
- You don't [do not] have a bicycle. (negative)
- Do you have a bicycle? (question)

Do another example or two if students seem to be having trouble. If they are having a lot of trouble, use the following sentences for more practice, then end the grammar exercise here.

- Peter plays baseball after school.
  Peter doesn't play baseball after school.
  Does Peter play baseball after school?

- Cesar goes to work early.
  Cesar doesn't go to work early.
  Does Cesar go to work early?

- They read a lot of books.
  They don't read a lot of books.
  Do they read a lot of books?

- You live close to Samira.
  You don't live close to Samira.
  Do you live close to Samira?

If students understand the basics of making a negative sentence and a question with the helping verb *do*, continue with the grammar exercise.

Using *Don't/Doesn't* in a Negative Statement

Point to the negative statement "You don't have a bicycle." Ask the students what words come before and after the contraction *don't*. (The subject and the verb.) Emphasize that this negative statement is not a question. Tell them they can also use *don't* and *doesn't* in questions, but in a question, these words will come at the beginning of the sentence.

Using *Don't* to Express Surprise and Doubt

When a question starts with *don't* or *doesn't*, it is generally an exclamation of surprise. The intonation of your voice goes up at the end of the question. Demonstrate the upward intonation of this question.

- **Don't** you have a bicycle? (No, I don't.)

In the lesson text today, Pilate asked Jesus: "Don't you hear what crimes they say you have done?" Write the question on the board. Ask the students what answer they think Pilate wanted Jesus to give.

Pilate was not asking if Jesus heard and understood the crimes people said he had done. Jesus had heard his accusers. By using the contraction *don't* at the beginning of a question, Pilate was expressing surprise that Jesus was not responding. He wanted Jesus to say, "Yes, I have heard them."

Using *don't* to begin a question is a way to express surprise at another person's reaction to a situation. Below are more examples.

- "**Don't** you honestly believe it pays to obey him?" (Job 35:3)

- "**Don't** you know that we all have God as our Father?" (Malachi 2:10)

- "'**Don't** you know?' he asked. 'No sir, I don't,' was my answer."
  (Zechariah 4:13)

In each of these verses, the person who asks the question is surprised that his listener doesn't know the answer or is surprised that the listener doesn't agree with the speaker's opinion.

Ask the students to think of some questions that begin with the word *don't*. Write them on the board and discuss them as a class. During this discussion, students might suggest sentences that seem rude to the listener ("Don't you know?" or "Don't you care?"). Explain that intonation and intent are important when starting a question with a negative contraction. There is more emotion packed into a "Don't you ..." question than into a normal question, so students should be sure to speak calmly, using these questions to express surprise and not criticism.

For Extra Practice

If your students seem comfortable with the idea of *don't* beginning a question that expresses surprise, you might tell them that other negative contractions of helping verbs can do the same job. Write the following examples on the board and ask what answer is expected.

- "**Aren't** you worth much more than birds?" (Matthew 6:26)
  Answer: Yes, I am.

- "**Don't** you know? **Haven't** you heard? **Hasn't** it been clear since the time of creation?" (Isaiah 40:21)
  Answer: Yes, I know. Yes, I have heard. Yes, it has been clear.

- "**Didn't** the one God create each of us?" (Malachi 2:10)
  Answer: Yes, He did.

Using *Don't* to Begin an Imperative Sentence

If your students are not familiar with the imperative mood yet, skip this section. However, if you have more intermediate students, you could review another way to use a negative contraction at the beginning of a sentence. Write the following on the board.

- "Don't be afraid of people." (Matthew 10:28)

Ask the following questions.

1. What kind of sentence is this? (imperative)
2. Where is the subject? (In an imperative sentence, the subject is *you*, but the word isn't present in the sentence because it is implied. In an imperative sentence, you are typically speaking to one person or a group of people.)

Tell the class that negative imperative sentences begin with *don't*. Write the following examples on the board:

- **Don't** eat those cookies. They are for the party.
- **Don't** turn on the TV. Martha is sleeping.
- **Don't** wear your boots in the house.

Ask them to think of more examples of imperative sentences that begin with *don't*.

For writing today, let's review questions that begin with *don't*. If you did not cover this topic, the worksheet in Appendix G can substitute for the writing exercise today, or you can ask students to write sentences using the preposition *against*.

Put students in pairs for this activity. Write the following question beginnings on the board.

- Don't you eat
- Don't you go
- Don't you like

Let students write these phrases in their notebooks and work in pairs to think of a way to finish the questions. Monitor their progress and answer questions for three to five minutes. Ask for a volunteer from each pair to write their best sentence on the board. Make corrections as needed.

If you would also like to do this activity with imperative statements, below are two sentence starters to use, or use some that the students have suggested.

- Don't go
- Don't forget to

Lesson 13

The Death Sentence

During Passover the governor always freed a prisoner chosen by the people. At that time a well-known terrorist named Jesus Barabbas was in jail. So when the crowd came together, Pilate asked them, "Which prisoner do you want me to set free? Do you want Jesus Barabbas or Jesus who is called the Messiah?" Pilate knew the leaders had brought Jesus to him because they were jealous.

While Pilate was judging the case, his wife sent him a message. It said, "Don't have anything to do with that innocent man. I have had nightmares because of him."

But the chief priests and the leaders convinced the crowds to ask for Barabbas to be set free and for Jesus to be killed. Pilate asked the crowd again, "Which of these two men do you want me to set free?"

"Barabbas!" they shouted.

Pilate asked them, "What am I to do with Jesus, who is called the Messiah?"

They all yelled, "Nail him to a cross!"

Pilate answered, "But what crime has he done?"

"Nail him to a cross!" they yelled even louder.

Pilate saw that there was nothing he could do and that the people were starting to riot. So he took some water and washed his hands in front of them and said, "I won't have anything to do with killing this man. You are the ones doing it!"

Everyone answered, "We and our own families will take the blame for his death!"

Pilate set Barabbas free. Then he ordered his soldiers to beat Jesus with a whip and nail him to a cross. (Matthew 27:15–26)

The Bible passage for this lesson is quite long, so it may take more time for the listening and reading sections. Because of this, the grammar section is a little shorter and we are combining pronunciation and spelling. To introduce this week's text, ask students to discuss the following questions.

- Have you ever had a dream, good or bad, that seemed real? Do you still remember the dream?
- Why do you think people make bad choices, even when they know they will have to pay the consequences?

Write the following comprehension questions on the board before you read to the class so students have an idea of what they are about to hear and have specific information to listen for.

- Why did the leaders bring Jesus to Pilate? (they were jealous)
- Who sent Pilate a message? (his wife)
- What did Pilate do with the water? (he washed his hands)

Read the passage to the students two or three times and ask them to answer the questions based on their listening.

Teach these words and expressions by writing them on the board, explaining their meanings, and asking the students to pronounce them after you. Then write the sample sentences on the board and have students repeat them after you several times.

1. free

(verb)—to allow somebody to leave prison or another place where they have been kept against their will (*Set free* is a phrasal verb with the same meaning.)
/**friː**/ or /**sɛt friː**/

"During Passover the governor always **freed** a prisoner chosen by the people." (Matthew 27:15)

"Pilate **set** Barabbas **free**." (Matthew 27:26)

2. come together

(phrasal verb)—individual parts that unite to make one thing
/**ˈkʌm** tə **ˈgɛ** ðər/

"God said, 'I command the water under the sky to **come together** in one place, so there will be dry ground.'" (Genesis 1:9)

"Many of the Lord's followers had **come together** there and were praying." (Acts 12:12)

3. nightmare

(noun)–a dream that is frightening or unpleasant (can also be used figuratively as in the second example)
/ˈnaɪt mer/

"During the second year that Nebuchadnezzar was king, he had such horrible **nightmares** that he could not sleep." (Daniel 2:1)

"Early evening, my favorite time, has become a **nightmare**." (Isaiah 21:4)

4. convince

(verb)–to make somebody (or yourself) believe that something is true
/kən ˈvɪns/

"Korah **had convinced** the rest of the Israelites to rebel against their two leaders." (Numbers 16:19)

"You **will be convinced** that I, the Lord God, was right in doing what I did." (Ezekiel 14:23)

5. take the blame

(expression)–accept responsibility for something bad or wrong that happens
/teɪk ðə bleɪm/

"Everyone answered, 'We and our own families will **take the blame** for his death!'" (Matthew 27:25)

"We'll **take the blame** if anyone who stays in this house gets hurt." (Joshua 2:17–20)

Reading
5–10 minutes

Hand out the Scripture passage written on paper, and let students read quietly to themselves for a few minutes. Ask if there are questions about anything they are reading. Read it out loud for the students at normal reading speed as they read along quietly. Since this passage is long, read it a second or third time.

Speaking
5–7 minutes

Review the Easter story up to this point. Ask students what they remember as you write a brief outline of the Easter story on the board. Students can refer to this outline during the speaking exercise.

Do a "Speed Speaking" activity. Have students form two lines and face a partner. Set a timer for one minute. The first student to speak will tell his or her partner the Easter story. When the timer goes off, the second person in the pair will speak for one minute. When these two minutes are up, one line moves a step to the right so that everyone has a new partner. Let them start again to tell the story of Easter. Repeat this process until everyone has spoken with at least three partners, or as long as interest holds. As they tell and retell the story, their confidence in the vocabulary and their speaking skills will improve.

Pronunciation Review

Let's practice spelling, speaking, and word linking with a sentence from the text. As students see the word and hear its pronunciation, they can learn spelling together with pronunciation this week.

Write the following sentence on the board. Read it to the students, then ask them to help you mark places in the sentence where they think words should be linked together.

- "I won't have anything to do with killing this man. You are the ones doing it!"

Read it together with the students, emphasizing and repeating in the places where students should link words together. (This is American English pronunciation.) It may sound something like this:

- "I won'ta vanything todo with killeen thi sman. Yoo-w-are the wunz doo-wee-nit!"

Word linking happens in all languages, including English. Of course, pronunciation varies with different English accents. Use the pronunciation that is common in the place where you and your students live. Remind students that the goal is not perfect English, because there is no such thing. The goal is to be understood and to understand.

The Short I Sound

The correct pronunciation of vowel sounds in American English is important. If a vowel sound is mispronounced, the meaning of the word can change significantly. The good news is that these sounds can be learned easily with practice and concentration when students speak.

Write the following words on the board, then pronounce them for the students.

bat, bet, bit, bot, but, bait, beet, bite, boat, boot, butte

All of these words have different meanings, and the only thing that changes in the pronunciation is the vowel sound. If your students are unfamiliar with the meaning of some of these words, pause and define them.

A Difficult Sound

The short *i* sound is not a common sound in other languages. Native speakers of romance languages, like Spanish, may have difficulty and will frequently substitute the long *e* sound. Write the following minimal pair on the board.

sit, seat

Pronounce the words in an exaggerated way for the students and point out the way your mouth position changes for each sound. With *seat*, the tip of the tongue stays behind the bottom front teeth, and the middle part of the tongue arches up toward the roof of the mouth but doesn't touch it. The sound is made in the front of the mouth. Your mouth will be wider than it is for the short i sound.

With *sit*, your jaw drops a little more than for long *e*. This means that the tongue isn't as close to the roof of your mouth. The tip of your tongue is forward and might touch the inside of the bottom front teeth. The sound is made in the middle of your mouth, and the lips stay relaxed. Let students practice saying these two words with you.

Practice with Short *I* and Long *E*

Write the following minimal pairs on the board, practice them together as a class, then silently point to a word and call on a student to pronounce the word that you are pointing to.

> hit, heat
> hill, he'll
> it, eat
> grin, green
> pill, peel
> his, he's
> still, steel
> fit, feet
> rich, reach

Tongue Twisters

Challenge your students with some tongue-twister sentences. Write the ones below on the board, say them for students, then have students say them with you. Call on several of the more vocal students to say the sentences, then ask for volunteers to try as well.

- I feel sick and ill after eating a big meal.
- Don't peel a peach or eat its pit.

If time allows, practice the following words with short *i* that appeared in our lesson text today.

prisoner, terrorist, in, which, is, him, his, it, with, innocent, convinced, killed, this, will, whip

Play Minimal Pairs Bingo

In Appendix H, you will find a Word Bingo game. The game is set up for short *i* and long *e* minimal pairs, but you can adapt it for any lesson where you feel studying minimal pairs would be helpful. This game also counts as the spelling exercise for this week.

To use a Bingo game with other minimal pairs, create your own free Bingo cards at https://myfreebingocards.com/.

Grammar

20 minutes

Grammar Review

Because this week's Scripture passage is long, many of the grammar topics we have already discussed appear in this lesson. Let's use today's text to reinforce some of the grammar that we talked about in lessons 1 through 5.

Make sure students have today's Scripture passage that you gave them during the reading exercise. Have a few extra copies ready. Put students in pairs or small groups for this grammar review. Monitor them as they work, and answer any questions. If many students seem to be having difficulty with one of the topics, just move on and take some time after the activity to review the material in the lesson that covered that topic.

If some students don't know the answers because they missed a class, encourage them to do the best they can with their groups. You could work with them individually later if you have time, but it's important to acknowledge the effort of students who do their best to attend class regularly.

Part 1. The Future Simple Tense

In lesson 1, we talked about the future simple tense. Ask students to find one place in today's Scripture passage that uses the future simple. Choose a volunteer to read the sentence out loud to the class. Ask the comprehension questions. Make sure all the groups agree about the answers before you continue to part 2.

Answer:
- "We and our own families will take the blame for his death!"

Ask students:
- Will they take the blame now? (no)
- Will they take the blame next year? (maybe or yes)
- Did they take the blame yesterday? (no)

Part 2. Prepositions of Location

In lesson 2, we talked about the prepositions *in, on,* and *at* as prepositions of location. Ask students to find two examples of *in* used as a preposition of location.

Answer:
- "At that time a well-known terrorist named Jesus Barabbas was **in** jail."
- "He took some water and washed his hands **in front of** them." (see Teacher Tip)

Teacher Tip

Students will probably choose this sentence as an example of the preposition *in*. However, the phrase *in front of* is technically a phrase that functions as a preposition of location. The prepositional phrase in this example is "in front of them." *Them* is the object of the preposition.

"In front of" as a preposition does not refer to an enclosed space, but to something that is ahead of, or facing something else. Explain to students that they can use this review session to learn a new preposition - *in front of.*

The goal is not to confuse students, even though English (and language study in general) can be confusing.

Students will most likely locate the same sentence (He washed his hands in front of them) as an example of the preposition *of* (in front of). They will want to know why this is incorrect. Just explain that in this case, *of* is part of a phrase that creates one preposition - *in front of* - as you discussed in the previous section.

Help them see this as learning a new preposition, instead of more confusing English grammar.

Remind students that the definition of *in* referred to "an enclosed space." How do these two uses of *in* describe an enclosed space? (inside the jail and enclosed on all sides; within the space that was "in front" of the crowd)

Part 3. The Preposition *Of*

In lesson 3, we talked about the preposition *of.* Ask students to find two places in the Scripture passage that use the preposition *of.*

Answer:
- "I have had nightmares because **of** him."
- "Which **of** these two men do you want me to set free?"
- "He took some water and washed his hands in front of them."
  (if students choose this sentence as an example of *of*, see Teacher Tip)

Remind students about the following two uses of *of* that they studied.

1. Who or what does it belong to?
2. What is it made from?

Ask students how *of* is used in these examples. (both show relationship— usage 1)

Part 4. The Preposition *To*

In lesson 4, we worked on the preposition *to.* Ask students to find three examples of *to* used as a preposition (after the verb) and three (there are more) examples of *to* used as part of the infinitive verb (before the verb).

Answer:

To used as a preposition:
- "Pilate knew the leaders had brought Jesus **to** him because they were jealous."
- "They all yelled, 'Nail him **to** a cross!'" (2x)
- "He ordered his soldiers to beat Jesus with a whip and nail him **to** a cross."

To used in the infinitive:
- "Which prisoner do you want me **to set** free?"
- "Don't have anything **to do** with that innocent man."
- "The chief priests and the leaders convinced the crowds **to ask** for Barabbas **to be** set free and for Jesus **to be** killed."
- "Which of these two men do you want me **to set free**?"
- "What am I **to do** with Jesus?"
- "The people were starting **to riot**."
- "I won't have anything **to do** with killing this man."
- "He ordered his soldiers **to** beat Jesus with a whip."

Part 5. Prepositions of Time

In lesson 5, we talked about *in, on*, and *at* as prepositions of time and included the preposition *during*. Ask students to find one example with *during* and one example with *at*.

Answer:

- "**During** Passover the governor always freed a prisoner chosen by the people."
- "**At** that time a well-known terrorist named Jesus Barabbas was in jail."

Writing

10–15 minutes

Ask the groups to write two sentences using the two prepositions of time that didn't appear in today's text—one sentence with *in* and one with *on*. Let volunteers come to the board and share their sentences. Make sure the sentences use these words as prepositions of time, not prepositions of location.

Ask students if there are any questions, and make sure they understand the differences between the prepositions as best you can. Reassure them that you will practice more in future classes.

The Story of Easter

Lesson 14

Soldiers Make Fun of Jesus

The governor's soldiers led Jesus into the fortress and brought together the rest of the troops. They stripped off Jesus' clothes and put a scarlet robe on him. They made a crown out of thorn branches and placed it on his head, and they put a stick in his right hand. The soldiers knelt down and pretended to worship him. They made fun of him and shouted, "Hey, you king of the Jews!" Then they spit on him. They took the stick from him and beat him on the head with it. (Matthew 27:27–30)

Introduce the Lesson
5–7 minutes

To introduce this week's Scripture passage, ask students to discuss the following questions. During speaking practice, remember not to correct students' grammar or pronunciation unless they ask for help. If they seem stuck, you can ask if they want help.

- Have you ever done something that was really difficult because you knew it would be good for somebody else?
- Why do you think people make fun (tease/say unkind things) of other people?

Listening Comprehension
10–15 minutes

Write the following comprehension questions on the board before you read to the class so students have an idea of what they are about to hear and have specific information to listen for.

- After the soldiers stripped off Jesus' clothes, what did they put on him? (a scarlet robe)
- What did the soldiers put in Jesus' right hand? (a stick)
- What part of Jesus' body did the soldiers beat with a stick? (his head)

Read the passage to the students two or three times and ask them to answer the questions based on their listening.

Vocabulary
10–15 minutes

We have four verbs today, so you could ask students to help you conjugate them in various tenses after you have discussed the meaning and pronunciation of each one. Two of them (*kneel* and *make fun*) are irregular. Be sure to have students repeat after you both the individual words and the sample sentences.

1. rest (of)
(noun)–the part of something that remains. Usually followed by the preposition *of*
/**rɛst**/

"So they stayed on for the **rest of** the day." (John 1:39)

"The **rest of** us went on ahead by ship." (Acts 20:13)

2. place
(verb)–to deliberately or carefully put something in or on a certain area or thing
/**pleɪs**/

"All nations will **place** their hope in him." (Matthew 12:21)

"Please come and **place** your hand on her. Then she will live again." (Matthew 9:18)

3. kneel
(verb)–a position where your body is supported on one or both knees
/**niːl**/

"I **kneel** in prayer to the Father." (Ephesians 3:14)

"Our Lord and our God, we praise you and **kneel** down to worship you, the God of holiness!" (Psalm 99:5)

4. pretend
(verb)–to behave in a way that makes other people believe something that is not true
/prɪ ˈtɛnd/

"They only **pretend** to be apostles of Christ." (2 Corinthians 11:13)

"When some people **pretended** to be apostles, you tested them and found out they were liars." (Revelation 2:2)

5. make fun (of)
(phrasal verb)–to say unkind things about somebody so that other people will laugh at them. Usually followed by the preposition *of*.
/**meɪk fʌn**/

"**Make fun of** wisdom, and you will never find it." (Proverbs 14:6)

"They **made fun of** Jesus and shouted, 'Hey, you king of the Jews!'" (Mark 15:18)

We are doing reading and speaking together today. Hand out a copy of the Scripture passage to each student. Give them some time to look at it, then read it once out loud for them as they read along silently.

Reading/ Speaking

10–15 minutes

Ask students to take turns reading out loud from the text. You could sit in a circle, and each student reads a sentence. The text could be broken down like this:

1. The governor's soldiers led Jesus into the fortress and brought together the rest of the troops.
2. They stripped off Jesus' clothes and put a scarlet robe on him.
3. They made a crown out of thorn branches and placed it on his head, and they put a stick in his right hand.
4. The soldiers knelt down and pretended to worship him.
5. They made fun of him and shouted, "Hey, you king of the Jews!"
6. They spit on him.
7. They took the stick from him and beat him on the head with it.

Go around the room several times so different students get a chance to read different sentences, some long and some short. Let students speak without correcting them, but encourage them if they correct themselves. Keep track of pronunciation errors made by more than one student. When the exercise is over, mention one or two of the most common problems and correct them as a group.

Silent *GH*

In today's lesson we have the word *brought*. English learners are frequently confused by silent letters, with good reason. The good news is that often when they see *gh*, it will be silent. However, it does make a sound sometimes, as in *laugh* and *ghost*. Let's take a closer look at *gh*.

Pronunciation

20 minutes

The digraph *gh* is not common, but students should be familiar with it. There are some rules, but for ESL learners, it's best to just learn the words individually as students come across them.

As you introduce these *gh* words, define any words that students do not know. However, make sure students know that they do not have to remember the meanings of all of these words. We are only studying the sounds of *gh*.

There will be a pronunciation exercise after we write all the words on the board, so write the words in groups according to their spelling. You could put them in columns in a chart as you write them on the board.

First group: silent *gh* followed by *t*

brought	night
caught	straight
sight	taught
thought	eight
daughter	

Ask students to help you define these words if the meanings are unfamiliar to them. Provide definitions if you need to. Ask the students to close their eyes. Say the words one by one, and ask students to repeat with their eyes closed so they cannot be reminded of how the word is spelled.

Students should understand that even though the spelling is difficult, the pronunciation is easy. Resist the temptation to write individual words phonetically—*tot* for *taught*, etc. Students need to become familiar with the way these words are spelled.

Second group: words with silent *gh* not followed by *t*

> though
> high
> neighbor
> dough
> sigh

Again, check that students know the definitions, then have them close their eyes and repeat the pronunciation after you.

Third group: *gh* pronounced as *f*

> enough
> laugh
> cough
> tough

Check that students know the definitions and have them repeat the pronunciation after you with their eyes closed.

Review

Now that you have all the words written on the board and have practiced them, point to each of them in random order and call on a student to say the word you are pointing to. Go through the words once or twice, depending on the size of your class. Each student should get to pronounce two or three times. Leave the words on the board for the next exercise.

Spelling/ Writing

15–20 minutes

Let's do writing and spelling together now, while these words are written on the board. Ask students to get out a pen and paper. Let them choose one (or two, if you have time) of the words on the board and write a sentence using that word. They should make sure everything is spelled correctly.

Pair students up and let them check each other's sentences. Ask for volunteers to come to the board and write their partner's sentences. This way, you may get more participation. Ask if it's okay to make corrections, then correct any spelling or grammar issues.

The Preposition *From*

Grammar will be the last section in today's lesson since we've already done writing.

Grammar

20 minutes

In today's text, the soldiers took the stick "from" Jesus. The preposition *from* has many meanings, but we are going to combine some of the most common usages into two sections:

1. "from" a physical location
2. "from" as an origin that is not a physical location

We'll also talk about a common expression with *from*.

1. From a Physical Location

The most common use of *from* is to describe the origin of someone or something. This is the easiest meaning of *from* for learners to understand. If you have beginners, just talk about the first meaning, *from* a physical location.

- "**From** Jerusalem and all Judea and **from** the Jordan River Valley crowds of people went to John." (Matthew 3:5)
  The people originated in Jerusalem and all Judea and the Jordan River Valley. They started there and came to John.

- "Answer their prayers **from** heaven and give them victory."
  (2 Chronicles 6:35)
  God is in heaven, and it is from there the answers to prayer will come.

Ask students to think of examples using a physical location where someone or something can be *from*. They may suggest sentences containing the phrasal verb *come from*, but as long as *come from* is followed by a physical location, it's okay to use for this exercise. Here are some ideas:

- I work with a man **from** Germany.
- Maria got a letter **from** home.
- Has the bus **from** Chicago arrived yet?
- This table is **from** the new furniture store.

If this is enough for your beginning students, stop here and do more practice by using these sentence starters. Write them on the board one by one. Students should orally suggest multiple possible endings to these sentences that use *from* to refer to a physical location.

- I live two blocks
- My grandparents are
- Roger is not
- He is
- The airplane _____ just landed.
- Olga just arrived on the bus

Teacher Tip

Come from is a common phrasal verb and is used differently than the preposition *from*.

A prepositional phrase with *from* can often be deleted from a sentence and the sentence will still be grammatically complete. However, you can't delete *from* if it is preceded by *come*, because you would be deleting part of the verb and the sentence would lose its meaning.

2. Origin That Is Not a Physical Location

We can also use *from* to describe the beginning or origin of things that are not physical locations. Here is an example:

- **"From** the day I was born, I have been in your care." (Psalm 22:10)

"The day I was born" is not a physical location, but it is a location in time. It is the origin or beginning of God's care for the psalmist. Below are more examples. Ask the students to tell you how *from* describes how something starts in these verses.

- "The women who knew how to make cloth **from** goat hair were glad to do so." (Exodus 35:26)
  The women were able to make cloth using the goat hair as a starting point.

- "Rachel and Leah said to Jacob: There's nothing left for us to inherit **from** our father." (Genesis 31:14)
  Their father was the source or origin of the things Rachel and Leah could have inherited.

- "Our ancestors were wise, so learn **from** them." (Job 8:8)
  Their ancestors were one source or origin of wisdom.

Prepositional Phrases with *From*

Like all prepositions, *from* will be followed by a noun or noun phrase, creating a prepositional phrase that adds more information to a sentence. Write the following example on the board.

- I received a letter **from** my brother.

Ask the students to:

1. Find the subject (I)
2. Find the verb (received)
3. Find the object (a letter)

The sentence is complete without the prepositional phrase "from my brother," but this phrase adds information about where this letter originated. Here is another example:

- Those pineapples are from Hawaii.

Ask students to:

1. Find the subject (pineapples)
2. Find the verb (are)
3. Find the object (In this case, because we are using the verb *be*, the object is the entire prepositional phrase *from Hawaii.*)

Teacher Tip

When the verb is a form of *be*, as in this sentence where the pineapples *are* from Hawaii, the prepositional phrase starting with *from* is generally the object of the sentence and is necessary for the sentence to make sense.

With other verbs, like *received*, the prepositional phrase is not normally necessary to create a complete sentence; e.g. "I received a letter."

The Story of Easter

Common Expression: *From ... To*

It is common to hear *from* used in an expression that shows the beginning and ending of an action in time. For example:

- The store is open **from** 10:00 a.m. **to** 8:00 p.m.
- We will be on vacation **from** Monday **to** Friday.

Ask students to suggest more examples with the expression *from ... to*.

The Difference Between *Of* and *From*

In many languages, one word can mean both *of* and *from*. However, English has two separate words, which can cause confusion for English learners.

Of in English is generally used in a possessive way, as we learned in lesson 3. Write the following example on the board:

- "The king **of** Egypt won't listen." (Exodus 11:9)

Explain that even though the king is "from" Egypt, he is also the king "of" Egypt. You could say that Egypt possesses him as its king. *Of* generally has this kind of possessive meaning.

We don't use *of* to describe the origin of someone or something. We use *from*. Below is another example. Write it on the board.

- "This is Jesus, the prophet **from** Nazareth." (Matthew 21:11)

Jesus is *from* Nazareth. Nazareth did not possess Jesus, like Egypt "possessed" its king. In many other languages, someone is "of" a place. In English, when we need to say the origin of a person, we say *from*.

Here's another example of the difference between *of* and *from*. Ask your intermediate students if the following sentences mean the same thing or not. If students think the sentences mean two different things, ask them if they can explain the difference.

- The box was made **from** bamboo.
- The box was made **of** bamboo.

When we use *from*, we are saying that bamboo was the origin of what the box was made from. It may not be obvious that bamboo was used to make the box. When we use *of*, we are saying that we see the bamboo. It is obvious that bamboo was used to make the box.

You could also refer back to the verse about making cloth from goat hair. *From* is used in that verse because once the goat hair had been made into cloth, it wasn't recognizable as goat hair anymore.

Quick Quiz

Below is the verse from today's lesson with the preposition *from*. Ask students to describe how it is being used as a preposition of origin in this phrase. Write it on the board.

- "They took the stick **from** him."
  (*From* is being used with the first meaning of a physical origin. The stick started in Jesus' hand, and the soldiers took the stick "from" his hand.)

Worksheet

Take some time to do the worksheet in Appendix I that asks students to choose the correct preposition, *of* or *from*. Let them work independently, then pair them up to check their answers. Ask for volunteers to give you the correct answers.

Jesus Is Nailed to a Cross

When the soldiers had finished making fun of Jesus, they took off the robe. They put his own clothes back on him and led him off to be nailed to a cross. On the way they met a man named Simon who was from Cyrene, and they forced him to carry Jesus' cross.

They came to a place named Golgotha, which means "Place of a Skull." There they gave Jesus some wine mixed with a drug to ease the pain. But when Jesus tasted what it was, he refused to drink it.

The soldiers nailed Jesus to a cross and gambled to see who would get his clothes. Then they sat down to guard him. Above his head they put a sign that told why he was nailed there. It read, "This is Jesus, the King of the Jews." The soldiers also nailed two criminals on crosses, one to the right of Jesus and the other to his left.

People who passed by said terrible things about Jesus. They shook their heads and shouted, "So you're the one who claimed you could tear down the temple and build it again in three days! If you are God's Son, save yourself and come down from the cross!"

The chief priests, the leaders, and the teachers of the Law of Moses also made fun of Jesus. They said, "He saved others, but he can't save himself. If he is the king of Israel, he should come down from the cross! Then we will believe him. He trusted God, so let God save him, if he wants to. He even said he was God's Son." The two criminals also said cruel things to Jesus. (Matthew 27:31–44)

To introduce this week's Scripture passage, put students in pairs or small groups. Write the following questions on the board and ask students to discuss them.

- It seems that people either loved Jesus or hated him.
  Why do you think some people loved Jesus?
  Why do you think some people hated him?

Give students three or four minutes, then come back together as a class. Ask for volunteers to tell how their groups answered each question.

Write the following comprehension questions on the board before you read to the class so students have an idea of what they are about to hear and have specific information to listen for. They only have to say whether each statement is true or false.

- After the soldiers removed the robe, they dressed Jesus in his own clothes. (true)
- A man named Simon was sent to bring wine for Jesus. (false)
- The sign above Jesus' head said, "This is Jesus, the king of the Jews." (true)
- People who came by were sad and spoke of the good things Jesus did. (false)
- The chief priests, leaders, and teachers of the Law of Moses said that Jesus had saved others. (true)

Read the verses to the students two or three times and ask them to answer the questions based on their listening. You may wish to take a vote after each question, see who thinks it is true or false, and discuss any disagreement. Read the passage again if necessary.

Today's words are mostly verbs that you can practice conjugating with your class once you have discussed the meaning and pronunciation. You will also be introducing the word *own* to your students. *Own* has different meanings and uses, but in today's lesson it is an adjective when preceded by a possessive noun or pronoun and followed by a noun.

1. own
(adjective)–used to emphasize that something belongs to or is connected with a particular person
(possessive noun or pronoun + **own** + noun)
/əʊn/

"Everyone had to go to their **own** hometown to be listed." (Luke 2:3)

"Even Jesus' **own** brothers had not yet become his followers." (John 7:5)

2. carry

(verb)–to support the weight of somebody or something and take it to another place
/ˈkæ ri/

"If a soldier forces you to **carry** his pack one kilometer, carry it two kilometers." (Matthew 5:41)

"We each must **carry** our **own** load." (Galatians 6:5)

3. come to

(phrasal verb)–to arrive at a particular place, or to reach a particular conclusion
/kʌm tu/

"Go out to the street corners and tell everyone you meet to **come to** the banquet." (Matthew 22:9)

"All their plans to harm you will **come to** nothing." (Psalm 21:11)

4. refuse

(verb)–to say or show that you will not do something that somebody has asked you to do
/rɪ ˈfjuːz/

"They asked him to stay longer, but he **refused**." (Acts 18:20)

"Everything I have told you is true, and you still **refuse** to have faith in me." (John 8:45)

5. trust

(verb)–to believe that someone or something is good, honest, etc. and will not try to harm or trick you
/trʌst/

"I **trust** you completely." (2 Corinthians 7:4)

"He **trusted** God, so let God save him, if he wants to." (Matthew 27:43)

Hand out the Scripture passage written on paper and let students read it quietly to themselves for three or four minutes. Ask if there are questions about anything they are reading.

This is a long passage with dialogue. After the students have read it silently to themselves, read out loud to the students as they read along. Be sure to demonstrate proper intonation. Highlight the fact that when you say a simple statement, the intonation of your voice will normally go down at the end of the sentence. When you say an exclamation, your intonation normally also goes down. But when you ask a question, the intonation of your voice usually goes up. Read the passage a second time as students listen to the intonation of your voice.

Practice proper intonation by asking the students to repeat the following simple phrases after you.

- I feel like having a hamburger for dinner. ↓
- Can we have hamburgers for dinner? ↑
- I love hamburgers! ↓

Speaking

5–7 minutes

For speaking today, let's do more practice with intonation. Explain that people express emotion and attitudes through intonation in their speech. Now that the students have heard a few examples, they can practice using intonation to express their own emotions and attitudes.

First, we'll imagine that we are saying the simple word *no*. Demonstrate that the way you say the word can add emotion and even meaning to what you say. Say the word *no* with a different intonation each time and ask the students to identify the emotion and/or meaning you are communicating. To help students remember the lesson, you could bring black socks to class and use them as a prop.

- No. (neutral intonation—you are just stating a fact.)
  Those socks are blue, not black.

- No. (falling intonation—the answer is obviously *no*.)
  Put those blue socks down; you need black socks.

- No? (rising intonation—why don't you agree with me?)
  You really think those socks are black?

- No! (authoritative, falling intonation, a command to stop.)
  Do not wear those black socks!

- No! (forceful, falling intonation, stop because what you are doing is dangerous.)
  Don't touch that hot stove!

- No? (uncertain, rising intonation, indicating that you thought something was correct, but you were wrong.)
  Oh, I see, those socks really are black.

- No! (disbelief, falling intonation—you are surprised that something you believed is not true.)
  I can't believe you were right about those socks and I was wrong.

Let students take turns using the word *no* with different intonations. Write the following sentences on the board and see if students can pronounce the word *no* with the proper intonation for the situation. The same sentence may be pronounced in different ways according to the speaker's intent.

- No, that's not what I meant.
- No, don't run into the street!
- No, you have to work at noon, remember?
- No, it's not dinnertime yet.
- No, I thought you told me to wait.
- No, I can't believe I missed the bus!
- No, it's okay.

Pronouncing the Consonant Pair *F* and *V*

Pronunciation

20 minutes

The consonant pair *f* and *v* can be confused quite often by English learners. For example, students whose native language is Arabic may have difficulty because there is no *v* sound in that language.

However, the fix should be simple, with practice, because *f* and *v* have the same mouth position. *F* is voiceless, using only air. *V* is voiced, so the vocal cords are added to produce this sound. Write the following words on the board.

off
of

Demonstrate the pronunciation of *off*, highlighting the position of your lips and teeth, with mouth in a relatively small *o* position, then moving your teeth to touch your lower lip slightly so that air can still pass through. Ask students to repeat.

Demonstrate the pronunciation of *of*, showing the same mouth position but adding your voice. Students should be able to place their hands on their necks and feel their vocal cords vibrating. Repeat *off* and *of* several times.

Practicing *F* and *V*

Let's use some minimal pairs to practice these sounds. Write the following words on the board.

belief	believe
fan	van
fine	vine
safe	save

Practice these words with students repeating after you. If you feel they are succeeding, point to one of the words on the board and call on individual students to say them.

Tongue Twisters

Try these tongue twisters with *f* and *v*. Write them on the board, demonstrate them slowly, then ask students to repeat after you.

- I have five knives and four forks.
- Fifty families on vacation feasted on vegetables, waffles, and French fries.

Spelling the F Sound

Remind students that in lesson 14 they learned that the *f* sound can also be spelled with *gh*. It can also be spelled with *ph,* and we will learn more about that in lesson 17. Write the following sample words on the board and practice their pronunciation with the class.

enough, phone, cough, pharmacy, laugh, alphabet

Remind students that they should be practicing these sounds outside of class. If they speak English as often as possible, their pronunciation will improve.

Spelling

10 minutes

Erase everything written on the board. Ask students to get out a pen and paper. Dictate the five vocabulary words to the students and three of the words with *f* spelled with *gh* or *ph*. For two bonus points, ask them to use two of the spelling words in sentences (a total of ten possible points). Students can pair up and exchange papers to check each other's work. See who earned the most points, and let a few volunteers write a sentence on the board to check grammar.

Grammar

20 minutes

Review of Preposition *From*

As a review, ask students to look through the verses on today's reading sheet to find the preposition *from* which they learned in the last lesson. Ask them to decide if it is being used to talk about physical locations/origin or if it is being used to talk about the cause of something. The answers are all physical location/origin.

Answers:

- "On the way they met a man named Simon who was **from** Cyrene."
- "If you are God's Son, save yourself and come down **from** the cross!"
- "If he is the king of Israel, he should come down **from** the cross!"

Reflexive Pronouns

We use reflexive pronouns when the subject and the object of the sentence are the same or refer to the same thing. *Myself* is a reflexive pronoun. Write it on the board. Ask if students are familiar with reflexive pronouns. If some students have studied them before, ask them to help you complete the list. The reflexive pronouns are:

- myself
- yourself
- himself
- herself
- itself

- ourselves (plural)
- yourselves (plural)
- themselves (plural)

There are two examples of reflexive pronouns in today's lesson. Write the following short sentence on the board.

- "He can't save himself."

Break the sentence down with the students.

1. Ask them what the subject is. (*he*, referring to Jesus)
2. Ask them what the verb is. (*save; can't save* could also be considered correct)
3. Ask them what the object is, who or what is receiving the action of the verb (Jesus, though it is not explicitly stated in the sentence)

In this verse, the Pharisees and teachers of the law expected Jesus to save Jesus, if he really was the Son of God. We can use the reflexive pronoun *himself* because the person doing the action and the person receiving the action are the same.

Write the following phrase on the board.

- Jesus can't save Jesus.

Say, "Instead of saying that ..." Erase the name Jesus and write "himself." Say, "It sounds better to say this:"

- Jesus can't save **himself**.

We've used the reflexive pronoun *himself* to replace the proper noun Jesus. This eliminates repetition and makes the sentence easier to read.

An Example in the Imperative Mood

The second example from today's Scripture passage is in the imperative mood. Even if students have not studied the imperative mood previously, they are probably familiar with what it is and what it is used for. Explain that in an imperative sentence, the subject is *understood*, or not mentioned in the sentence. In the following example, the comment is spoken directly to Jesus, so he is the understood subject of this sentence. Write this short sentence on the board.

- "Save yourself and come down from the cross!"

Ask students to tell you where the subject is.(There is no stated subject because this is an imperative sentence.)

In this example, the people who passed by said this directly to Jesus, so it can be inferred that the subject of this imperative sentence is *you*, meaning Jesus.

- **You** save **yourself** and come down from the cross!

Below are the pronouns and adjectives that refer to people and things.

Subject pronouns
I, you, he/she/it, we, you (plural), they

Object pronouns
me, you, him/her/it, us, you (plural), them

Possessive pronouns
mine, yours, his, hers, its, ours, yours (plural), theirs

Possessive adjectives
(followed by a noun)
my, your, his/her/its, our, your (plural), their

Reflexive pronouns
myself, yourself, himself/herself/itself, ourselves, yourselves, themselves

The reflexive pronoun *yourself* is used because the people were asking Jesus to save Jesus, to save himself. The subject and the object of this sentence are the same, so we can use a reflexive pronoun in the object to refer back to the subject.

Below are a few more examples of reflexive pronouns. Ask students to identify the subject, verb, and object (reflexive pronoun) in each sentence. Also ask them to locate the example that is imperative.

- "Don't brag about **yourself**—let others praise you." (Proverbs 27:2)
  Imperative: You / don't brag / about yourself.

- "She had said to **herself**, 'If I can just touch his clothes, I will be healed.'"
  (Mark 5:28)
  She / said / to herself

- "Jesus replied: If you had faith no bigger than a tiny mustard seed, you could tell this mulberry tree to pull **itself** up, roots and all, and to plant **itself** in the ocean. And it would!" (Luke 17:6)
  mulberry tree / pull / itself
  mulberry tree / plant / itself

- "We have kept **ourselves** pure and have been understanding, patient, and kind." (2 Corinthians 6:6)
  we / have kept / ourselves

- "Some of you call **yourselves** Jews." (Romans 2:17)
  you / call / yourselves

Depending on the skill level of your class, you can stop here and do the worksheet in Appendix J, questions 1–7.

Reflexive Pronouns Used for Emphasis

We can add a reflexive pronoun to a sentence for emphasis. Below are some examples to write on the board.

- "While everyone else was being baptized, Jesus **himself** was baptized."
  (Luke 3:21)

- "Jacob **himself** walked in front of them all." (Genesis 33:3)

- "I am signing this letter **myself**: PAUL." (Colossians 4:18)

If we eliminate the reflexive pronouns, the sentences would be:

- While everyone else was being baptized, Jesus was baptized.

- Jacob walked in front of them all.

- I am signing this letter: PAUL.

The reflexive pronoun is included to add emphasis. Ask the students if they think that adding a reflexive pronoun for emphasis makes the sentence more interesting or emotional.

By Myself

Reflexive pronouns are often used with the preposition *by* to indicate that someone was alone in some way. It is possible to delete these phrases from a sentence without losing meaning, but they give the sentence more interest and detail.

Write the following examples on the board. First write them without *by myself* and *by himself*. Then add the phrases to the sentence so students can see how they add emphasis.

- "How can I take care of all these people **by myself**?" (Numbers 11:14)

- "Later in the evening he was still there **by himself**." (Mark 6:47)

Give each student a copy of the worksheet in Appendix J. They should choose the reflexive pronoun that fits best in the sentence. Beginners can do questions 1 to 7. Questions 8 to 10 cover the additional information that was included for more advanced learners.

Write the following sentence starters on the board. Put students into pairs to write two sentences using reflexive pronouns. They can write their own or use these sentence starters. Let them work for three minutes or choose a reasonable amount of time for your students to finish the work.

Writing
10–15 minutes

1. I usually _____ by myself.
2. She _____ in the mirror.
3. You should _____ more often.

Assign two of the pairs (a total of four students) to work together and finish or correct the sentences they have written. Let a representative from each group orally share the best sentence with the class.

The Story of Easter

Lesson 16

The Death of Jesus

At noon the sky turned dark and stayed that way until three o'clock. Then about that time Jesus shouted, *"Eli, Eli, lema sabachthani?"* which means, "My God, my God, why have you deserted me?"

Some of the people standing there heard Jesus and said, "He's calling for Elijah." One of them at once ran and grabbed a sponge. He soaked it in wine, then put it on a stick and held it up to Jesus.

Others said, "Wait! Let's see if Elijah will come and save him." Once again Jesus shouted, and then he died.

At once the curtain in the temple was torn in two from top to bottom. The earth shook, and rocks split apart. Graves opened, and many of God's people were raised to life. They left their graves, and after Jesus had risen to life, they went into the holy city, where they were seen by many people.

The officer and the soldiers guarding Jesus felt the earthquake and saw everything else that happened. They were frightened and said, "This man really was God's Son!"

Many women had come with Jesus from Galilee to be of help to him, and they were there, looking on at a distance. Mary Magdalene, Mary the mother of James and Joseph, and the mother of James and John were some of these women. (Matthew 27:45–56)

To introduce this week's Scripture passage, make a simple mind map with the students. Write the word "miracle" in large letters in the middle of the board. Provide the dictionary definition. (Oxford Learner's Dictionary defines *miracle* as "an act or event that does not follow the laws of nature and is believed to be caused by God.")

Introduce the Lesson

5–7 minutes

Ask the students what words come to their minds when they hear the word *miracle*. (If they need inspiration, write *surprise, wonder, unusual,* or *God*.) Write their ideas on the board around the word *miracle*. Connect these words to the keyword *miracle* with lines, like a sunburst. The connecting words don't have to be correct or accurate, because they are simply the words that your students may think of, and not necessarily in English. You may need to help them with translations.

Now write this question on the board:

- Have you ever experienced something that you thought was a miracle?

Let a couple of students share with the class. If nobody has any ideas, share another of God's miracles with them, such as Daniel in the lions' den.

Listening Comprehension
10–15 minutes

Write the following comprehension questions on the board before you read to the class so students have an idea of what they are about to hear and have specific information to listen for.

- What time did the sky turn dark? (noon)
- What did someone offer Jesus to drink? (wine)
- What part of the temple was torn in two from top to bottom? (the curtain)
- How did the soldiers feel when they saw everything that was happening? (frightened)

Read the Scripture passage to the students two or three times and ask them to answer the questions based on their listening.

Vocabulary
10–15 minutes

This passage has a lot of vocabulary that your students may not be familiar with. Feel free to substitute the words your students need in place of the words that are listed here. Possibilities for more vocabulary include *split apart, shout, stick, sponge,* etc.

The word *desert* (meaning "to leave someone without help or support") will be interesting, because it is both a homophone and a homograph (DE-sert (meaning "a dry, arid place"), de-SERT, and des-SERT (meaning "a sweet treat at the end of a meal"). You might want to introduce these variations to your class if they like to know these sorts of things and would enjoy it.

1. turn (become)
(linking verb)–to become, to change into a new form or condition
(Many times it is used as a phrasal verb with the preposition *into* and has the same meaning.)
/tɜːrn/

"On the way, Lot's wife looked back and was **turned** into a block of salt."
(Genesis 19:26)

"God **turns** darkness to light." (Job 12:22)

2. desert
(verb)–to leave someone without help or support
/də ˈzɜːrt/

"You are the Lord God! Stay nearby and don't **desert** me." (Psalm 38:21)

"The Lord has promised that he will not leave us or **desert** us." (Hebrews 13:5)

3. grab
(verb)–to use your hands to take somebody or something and hold it quickly or roughly
/ɡræb/

"They **grabbed** Paul and dragged him out of the temple." (Acts 21:30)

"One of them ran and **grabbed** a sponge." (Mark 15:36)

4. curtain
(noun)–a piece of cloth that covers a window or other opening
/ˈkɜːr tən/

"Behind the **curtain** was the most holy place." (Hebrews 9:3)

"And this way takes us through the **curtain** that is Christ himself." (Hebrews 10:20)

5. soak
(verb)–to put something in liquid for a time so it becomes completely wet
/soʊk/

"At night my bed and pillow are **soaked** with tears." (Psalm 6:6)

"He slept outside where his body was **soaked** with dew." (Daniel 5:21)

Teacher Tip
What are *homophones, homographs, and homonyms?*

Homophone
Homo means "same," and *phone* means "sound," so homophones are words that sound alike. They may have different meanings and spellings, or they may be spelled the same way. Examples are *by, buy, and bye*, and *bark* (of a tree) and *bark* (the sound a dog makes).

Homograph
Graph means "writing." *Homographs* are words that are spelled the same but have different meanings. Examples are *bear* (to carry) and *bear* (the animal).

Homonym
A general definition for *homonym* is "words that sound the same but have different meanings." Some experts believe *homonyms* are both homophones and homographs, and others think the word *homonym* can refer to one or the other as well as both.

Pass out a copy of this rather long passage and let the students read through it silently to themselves for one minute. If they are unable to finish, tell them that's okay and that they will have another opportunity to read soon.

Explain that reading has fluency too, just like speaking. Even though English is only in a student's thoughts as they read to themselves, the more fluent their reading is, the more they will enjoy it and want to read more.

Reading contains something called "sight words." These are common words that we don't have to think about the meaning of as we read. They allow for speed and accuracy, which is fluency.

Reading

10–15 minutes

Sight words are learned over time. The longer someone has studied English, the more familiar they will be with many of these sight words. The more your students practice reading, the more sight words they will learn and remember.

Here is a list of many of the sight words in today's text. Write them one by one on the board (it may take a while), say them, and ask students to repeat. Practice them more as a group by pointing to a word on the board and calling on a student to say it.

a, after, again, and, at, be, for, from, had, have, he, him, if, in, into, it, many, me, my, of, on, once, one, said, some, that, the, their, them, then, there, these, they, this, three, to, two, until, up, was, were, where, which, why, will, with, you

This is quite a list! And many of these words are repeated more than once. Encourage your students that they really do have reading skills. By learning a few new vocabulary words each day or each week, their reading will improve dramatically as they confidently practice.

Let them read the Scripture passage quietly to themselves to see if they can read it faster after having practiced the sight words.

Pronunciation/
Speaking

20 minutes

Sight Words

Today we are going to do pronunciation and speaking together.

In lesson 2, we discussed how unstressed words are "reduced," or pronounced differently from how they are spelled. This is because native English speakers keep a similar gap of time between stressed words. Any unstressed words that happen to be between these stressed words change or shorten their pronunciation in order to maintain this rhythm.

Many sight words fall into this category of unstressed words. However, sight words like adjectives (the numbers two and three), verbs (said and have), and adverbs (where and why) will still normally be stressed in a sentence.

Below are some of the sight words (in bold) as they appear in one of the verses we read today.

- **He** soaked **it in** wine, **then** put **it on a** stick **and** held **it up to** Jesus.

Notice that the majority of the words in the sentence are sight words. In this sentence, the sight words are structure words that are normally unstressed in a sentence. They tend to change their pronunciation in relation to the words around them.

Read the sentence to the students. Bolded words are the unstressed sight words. Notice that you naturally stress the words that are not bold (nouns and verbs), and there is a similar interval of time in between each one. The structure words reduce and change pronunciation to fit inside this space between stressed words. Here's a sample pronunciation in American English:

- He soakedidin wine, then pudidona stick n heldidup| t'Jesus.

The "|" indicates that *p*, as a stop consonant, is not pronounced completely.

Ask students to repeat after you. Remind them how *t* becomes "flap t" between two vowels. They should have a little fun with this exercise, but it isn't required that they pronounce the words this way. If they choose to give each word its full pronunciation, they will be understood, though their English will not sound native-like.

If you have time and your students seem to enjoy this exercise, here's another sentence from today's text:

- At noon the sky turned dark and stayed that way until three o'clock.

Remember, the bold words are sight words and are usually unstressed, depending on the speaker's intention. If they are nouns or verbs, they retain their stress and get full pronunciation.

- Ut|noon th'sky turn'dark n stayed that| way ntil three uh'clock.

Now that you've reviewed the pronunciation of sight words, read the passage to the students again and ask them to focus on listening to the sight words. Let them notice if these short, unstressed words are pronounced differently than they would expect. Ask them to pair up and consciously think about reducing sight words as they read the passage out loud to each other.

Expressions with *Once*

Grammar
20 minutes

This grammar lesson will be a little shorter because we spent more time on reading and speaking. The spelling exercise at the end is optional if you have time.

At Once

Let's take a look at the expression *at once*, which appears twice in our text. By itself, *once* is an adverb that means "one time only." *Once* is also used in many expressions. It is combined with different words to create different meanings.

Write these sentences on the board:

- "One of them **at once** ran and grabbed a sponge."
- "**At once** the curtain in the temple was torn in two from top to bottom."

At once means "immediately, with no delay." Ask a volunteer to read each sentence you have written, substituting the word *immediately* for *at once*. Here are some more examples to write on the board:

- "He came to me and said, 'Saul, my friend, you can now see again!' **At once** I could see." (Acts 22:13)
- "**At once** they left the boat and their father and went with Jesus." (Matthew 4:22)

- "**All at once** Moses and Elijah were there talking with Jesus." (Matthew 17:3)

It's important to note that *at once* generally only appears in writing or formal conversation. In casual conversation, speakers generally say "right away" to mean the same thing as *at once*. Read the sentences again, substituting "right away" for "at once."

Sometimes *all at once* can mean "simultaneously" or "at the same time." Here is a verse with *all at once* used in this way.

- "That's why the Lord had not let Joshua get rid of those enemy nations **all at once**." (Judges 2:23)

Reinforce this meaning by asking a student to read the verse out loud to the class, substituting the words *at the same time* for *all at once* in this sentence.

Once Again

The expression *once again* means "one more time." Just like *at once*, it's a little more formal and not used much in informal conversation. It adds emphasis to the fact that something is happening again. In casual conversation, speakers would probably just say, "again."

Once again typically appears at the beginning of a sentence, while the more casual *again* will typically be at the end of a sentence. On the board, write the way it was used in today's text.

1. "**Once again** Jesus shouted, and then he died."

Ask the students to help you rewrite this sentence, changing "once again" into "again," then moving "again" to the end of the sentence. Here are some more examples.

2. "**Once again** Jesus got into the boat and crossed Lake Galilee." (Mark 5:21)

3. "I will make them into one nation and let them **once again** live in the land of Israel." (Ezekiel 37:22)

Answers:
1. Jesus shouted **again**, and then he died.
2. Jesus got into the boat and crossed Lake Galilee **again**.
3. I will make them into one nation and let them live in the land of Israel **again**.

Dictate the following sentence to the students at normal speed and with normal pronunciation. Say it a maximum of three times. Students should correctly spell all the words in the sentence, especially the sight words.

Spelling

5–8 minutes

"At once the curtain in the temple was torn in two from top to bottom."

Let students exchange papers and check their partners' work. Ask for volunteers to spell the vocabulary words for the class as you write them on the board. Ask for another volunteer to write the sentence on the board. Check as a class and correct any mistakes.

Practice using expressions with *once* by writing some sentences. Write the following sentence starters on the board if your students need some ideas.

Writing

10–15 minutes

- Once again, John went
- At once we
- All at once, the neighbor's dog

Put students into pairs or small groups to compare and check their sentences with each other, then ask for volunteers to share a sentence by writing it on the board. Make gentle corrections if necessary.

The Story of Easter

Lesson 17

Jesus Is Buried

That evening a rich disciple named Joseph from the town of Arimathea went and asked for Jesus' body. Pilate gave orders for it to be given to Joseph, who took the body and wrapped it in a clean linen cloth. Then Joseph put the body in his own tomb that had been cut into solid rock and had never been used. He rolled a big stone against the entrance to the tomb and went away.

All this time Mary Magdalene and the other Mary were sitting across from the tomb.

On the next day, which was a Sabbath, the chief priests and the Pharisees went together to Pilate. They said, "Sir, we remember what this liar said while he was still alive. He claimed in three days he would come back from death. So please order the tomb to be carefully guarded for three days. If you don't, his disciples may come and steal his body. They will tell the people he has been raised to life, and this last lie will be worse than the first one."

Pilate said to them, "All right, take some of your soldiers and guard the tomb as well as you know how." So they sealed it tight and placed soldiers there to guard it. (Matthew 27:57–66)

To introduce this week's text, write the following question on the board

- Why do children tell lies?

Let a few volunteers answer. Then write this question on the board:

- Why do adults tell lies?

Let a few students briefly share their thoughts.

> **Introduce the Lesson**
>
> 5–10 minutes

Write the following comprehension questions on the board before you read to the class so students have an idea of what they are about to hear and have specific information to listen for.

- What did Joseph of Arimathea ask for? (Jesus' body)
- Who gave the order to give Joseph what he asked for? (Pilate)
- Where were Mary Magdalene and the other Mary sitting (across from the tomb, near the tomb)
- What day did the chief priests go to Pilate? (the Sabbath, the next day)

Read the verse to the students two or three times and ask them to answer the questions based on their listening.

Write each vocabulary word on the board and pronounce it as you write the definition. Since all our words today are verbs, ask students to help you conjugate them in a few tenses, for use in the spelling exercise later today.

1. wrap
(verb)–to cover something completely in paper or another material
(The final *p* is doubled to spell the past simple tense—*wrapped*)
/**ræp**/

"During the meal Jesus got up, removed his outer garment, and **wrapped** a towel around his waist." (John 13:4)

"The sailors **wrapped** ropes around the ship to hold it together." (Acts 27:17)

2. roll
(verb)–to turn something over and over and move it in a particular direction
/r**oʊ**l/

"A stone was **rolled** over the pit, and it was sealed." (Daniel 6:17)

"He **rolled** the rock away and watered the sheep." (Genesis 29:10)

3. go away
(phrasal verb)–to leave a person or a place (In today's passage this phrasal verb appears in the past tense: *went away*.)
/**goʊ** ə ˈ**weɪ**/

"Now please ask him to make these snakes **go away**." (Numbers 21:7)

"Three times I begged the Lord to make this suffering **go away**."
(2 Corinthians 12:8)

4. claim

(verb)–to say that something is true even though it hasn't been proved and other people may not believe it

/**kleɪm**/

"Many will come and **claim** to be me." (Mark 13:6)

"They **claim** to be wise, but they are fools." (Romans 1:22)

5. seal

(verb)–to close a container tightly, especially so that air, liquid, etc. cannot get in or out

/**siːl**/

"My message and my teachings are to be **sealed** and given to my followers." (Isaiah 8:16)

"A stone was rolled over the pit, and it was **sealed**." (Daniel 6:17)

Pass out the Scripture passage written on paper for students. Let them look it over and read silently to themselves for a minute or two, being mindful of sight words that will make their reading more fluent.

Answer any questions about unknown vocabulary, as time allows. Read the text out loud as the students read along. Ask them to focus on listening to "sight words" and the rhythm of stressed and unstressed words.

Reading

5–10 minutes

The *F* Sound of *PH*

One of the easiest reading challenges for English learners is discovering that *ph* makes the *f* sound. It's easy because it is very predictable in common words that speakers use every day. There are very few exceptions, *shepherd* (shep-erd) being perhaps the most common.

There are two words in today's Scripture passage that have the *ph* pronounced as *f*, and students have probably seen them before: "Joseph" and "Pharisees." Write them on the board and pronounce them for the students. Underline the *ph* spelling and remind them of the mouth position for the *f* pronunciation that we studied in lesson 15. Students should repeat after you several times.

Write the following *ph* words on the board and let students go around the room a few times and pronounce them. Let students ask about any word they do not know the meaning of.

alphabet
physics
phone
nephew
prophecy

Pronunciation

20 minutes

philosophy

pharmacist

sphere

elephant

geography, photography and other words ending with -*graphy*

Add more to the list if you like. Words with *ph* tend to have a Latin origin, so students with first languages like Spanish or French will probably have something equivalent in spelling or pronunciation. These students may enjoy sharing how these words would be spelled in their language.

Speaking

5–7 minutes

We are getting close to the end of the Easter story. You have probably had students miss one or more classes, so they missed part of the story. In this speaking exercise, your students can help one another by telling what they remember about the story so far.

Ask for volunteers to tell one thing they remember from the Easter story— anything from last week's lesson all the way back to lesson 1. If students don't seem to remember or don't want to talk, ask them to describe some of the people from the story. Here are some sample questions:

- Who was Peter? What did he say he would never do?
- Who was Judas and what did he do?
- What do you remember about Jesus and the disciples in the garden of Gethsemane?
- Give your opinion of the Jewish priests and leaders. What kind of people were they?
- Who was Pilate?

In today's passage, Mary Magdalene and the other Mary were sitting across from the tomb, watching all these things taking place. Ask students to imagine the conversation these two women might have had. How might they have been feeling, knowing that Jesus had died? Let students share their thoughts with the class.

Spelling

5–8 minutes

We had five verbs in our vocabulary lesson today. Dictate these verbs in various tenses, like future simple and past simple, after reviewing these conjugations during the vocabulary exercise. Use a few of the *ph* words from the pronunciation section. Have students exchange papers with a partner to check, then write the correct spellings on the board and check them as a class.

Grammar

20 minutes

The Passive Voice

We have several examples of sentences in the passive voice in today's passage. When a sentence is written in the passive voice, the subject is not doing the action but having the action done to it by someone or something else. Let's talk more about the passive voice and how it might be useful for students to know and use themselves.

Write these sentences on the board:

1. Matthew wrote the story of Jesus.
2. The story of Jesus was written by Matthew.

Ask the students what is the same about the two sentences. They might say that the sentences mean the same thing or that they mention words that are common to both sentences, like "Matthew" and "the story of Jesus." Cross out the words that are the same in each sentence.

1. ~~Matthew~~ wrote ~~the story of Jesus.~~
2. ~~The story of Jesus~~ was written by ~~Matthew.~~

When we remove the words that are the same in each sentence, we are left with the verbs and one preposition *(by)*. Ask the students what tense the verb in sentence one is (past simple tense). Ask if they know how the verb in the second sentence is different (passive voice). See if the students can tell you how the meaning of the two sentences is different.

Active Voice

In sentence 1, the subject, Matthew, is performing the action of writing. "Matthew wrote." What did he write? The "story of Jesus," which is the object of the sentence.

Passive Voice

In sentence 2, the object of the sentence, or the thing that received the action, is the subject. By writing the sentence this way, we are saying that the subject of the sentence, the story of Jesus, is more important than who wrote it.

The best way to explain the passive voice is to stress what is important in each sentence. In the active voice, Matthew is more important than what he wrote. In the passive voice, the story of Jesus is more important than knowing who wrote it. The passive voice is useful when the verb and the object of the action are more important than who or what actually did the action.

Forming the Passive Voice

The passive voice is made by using a form of the verb *be* plus a past participle. Regular past participles are made by adding *-ed* to a verb, like *kick (kicked)* or *place (placed)*.

Unfortunately, many past participles are irregular. "Was written," from our example, is the verb *be* in the past tense and *written*, the irregular past participle of the verb *write*.

Teacher Tip

Students may be confused between the passive voice and the present perfect or past continuous since these have similar construction.

The **passive voice** uses the helping verb *be* and the main verb in the past participle *(-ed)* form.

• The homework was finished by John.

The **past continuous** also uses the helping verb *be* but uses the present participle *(-ing)* instead of the past participle *(-ed)*.

• John was finishing the homework.

The **present perfect** uses the helping verb *have* and the main verb in the past participle *(-ed)* form.

• John has finished the homework.

More Examples

Any verb tense can be made passive. Below is a compound sentence from our lesson today that uses the past perfect tense in the passive form. Write it on the board.

- Joseph put the body in his own tomb that had been cut into solid rock and had never been used.

The first part of the sentence is active and tells us that Joseph put the body in his own tomb. Erase that part of the sentence. The second part of the sentence uses passive verbs in the past perfect tense (see Teacher Tip) to describe the tomb.

- … that **had been cut** into solid rock …
- … and **had never been** used.

Ask the students, "Who cut the tomb into solid rock?" We don't know, and it isn't important. The only thing that matters is that the tomb was cut into solid rock. Ask the students, "Who never used the tomb?" It doesn't matter. All we need to know is that the tomb had never been used.

Optional Review Game

Past participles are used with the passive tense. If you would like to take some time and review irregular past participles, like *written*, you will find a list of the most common ones in Appendix K.

Play a game by giving each student a copy of the list and letting them review it for several minutes—no notetaking allowed. Then ask them to put the list away. Divide them into two teams, perhaps men against women. You call out a verb from the list for team 1 to name the past participle form. They have five seconds. Team 2 gets a turn if team 1 can't think of it or gets it wrong. The team that correctly says the irregular past participle gets a chance to come to the board and spell it correctly.

Call out a verb for team 2 and repeat the process. Teams get one point for naming the correct past participle and another point for spelling it correctly. Play as long as time allows, or to a certain point score, like 20 or 30 points.

For more practice with the passive voice, let's play a game for our writing exercise.

Practice as a Group

Before playing, practice as a large group by doing a few sample sentences. Write these sentences on the board:

- Our bread _____ using the best ingredients. (make)
- Those apartments _____ in 1990. (build)
- The package _____ tomorrow by 2:00. (deliver)

Writing

10–15 minutes

Using the verb in parentheses, ask students to help you create the passive voice.

1. Add the verb *be* in the correct tense.
2. Change the base verb into its past participle form. Note that the verbs *make* and *build* have irregular past participles.

Answers are:

- Our bread **is made** using the best ingredients. (present tense)
- Those apartments **were built** in 1990. (past tense)
- The package **will be delivered** tomorrow by 2:00. (future tense)

Playing the Game

Depending on the size of your class, divide students into groups so there are no more than three students per group. Give each group a copy of the game sheet from Appendix L. Playing the game in small groups ensures that everyone has more chances to participate and shortens the time needed to finish the game.

Students will roll a die and land on a square with a sentence and a base verb. They should change the verb to the passive voice so that it makes sense in the sentence. They can say it or write it down if they need time to think. If they are successful, they can stay on the space. If they are not successful, they have to return to their previous square and try again on their next turn. First student of each group to the end wins.

Circulate around the room as your groups play so you are available to monitor their answers and answer questions. The answers are on page 2 of Appendix L.

THE Story of Easter

Lesson 18

Jesus Is Alive

The Sabbath was over, and it was almost daybreak on Sunday when Mary Magdalene and the other Mary went to see the tomb. Suddenly a strong earthquake struck, and the Lord's angel came down from heaven. He rolled away the stone and sat on it. The angel looked as bright as lightning, and his clothes were white as snow. The guards shook from fear and fell down, as though they were dead.

The angel said to the women, "Don't be afraid! I know you are looking for Jesus, who was nailed to a cross. He isn't here! God has raised him to life, just as Jesus said he would. Come, see the place where his body was lying. Now hurry! Tell his disciples he has been raised to life and is on his way to Galilee. Go there, and you will see him. This is what I came to tell you."

The women were frightened and yet very happy, as they hurried from the tomb and ran to tell his disciples. Suddenly Jesus met them and greeted them. They went near him, held on to his feet, and worshiped him. Then Jesus said, "Don't be afraid! Tell my followers to go to Galilee. They will see me there." (Matthew 28:1–10)

There is a lot of fear in this week's story, yet we see that the women felt frightened and happy at the same time. Have a brief discussion with the students, and ask them these questions for thought:

- Think about a time when you or someone you know was afraid.
- What was the thing that made you or your friend afraid?
- How or why did you or your friend stop being afraid?

It isn't necessary for everyone to speak, because the purpose of this exercise is just to prepare them for what they are about to hear. Let a few volunteers share their thoughts with the class.

Introduce the Lesson

5–10 minutes

Write the following comprehension questions on the board before you read to the class. Read them out loud to the students and make sure they understand what each question is asking.

As you read, ask the students to raise their hands (no talking) when they hear the answer to the first question. Call on one of the students with a raised hand to tell you what they heard that made them think they had the right answer. Ask the rest of the students to raise their hands if they agree, and if there is disagreement, discuss together. If everyone agrees, continue reading.

When they hear the answer to the second question, they should raise their hands (no talking). Continue in this way through the five questions.

- What time of day did the women go to the tomb? (daybreak, morning)
- What happened to the ground before the angel appeared? (earthquake)
- What did the guards do when they saw the angel? (shook from fear, fell down)
- Why did the disciples need to go to Galilee? (to meet Jesus)
- When the women saw Jesus, what part of his body did they hold on to? (his feet)

Ask a sixth question verbally (not written on the board):

- What were the women told not to do, once by the angel and once by Jesus? (don't be afraid)

Read the passage a second time without any pauses as the students listen for the answer to the sixth question. If nobody knows the answer, read the text a third time.

Below are five new vocabulary words for this lesson. As usual, write them, pronounce the word and explain the meaning, and write sample sentences. Say the word, emphasizing the syllables, and have students repeat. Write and say the sentences, and have students repeat. For practice, ask students to help you change the verbs in the sample sentences to other tenses.

1. be over
(phrasal verb)–to be finished, come to an end
/bi ˈoʊ vər/

"After the battle **was over** that day ..." (Judges 5:1)

"Night **is** almost **over**, and day will soon appear." (Romans 13:12)

2. daybreak
(noun)–dawn, the time of day when light first appears.
/ˈdeɪ breɪk/

"At **daybreak** the king got up and ran to the pit." (Daniel 6:19)

"On the seventh day, the army got up at **daybreak**." (Joshua 6:15)

3. bright
(adjective)–full of light, shining strongly (Bright has many figurative as well as literal meanings.)
/**braɪt**/

"The world was made **bright** by lightning." (Psalm 77:18)

"You make my life pleasant, and my future is **bright**." (Psalm 16:6)

4. shake
(verb)–to move up and down or side to side with short, quick movements, or to make somebody or something else move in this way
/**ʃeɪk**/

"Moses started **shaking** all over and didn't dare to look at the bush." (Acts 7:32)

"Merely **shake** the trees, and fruit will fall into every open mouth." (Nahum 3:12)

5. hold on
(phrasal verb)–to continue to hold someone or something
/**hoʊld ɑːn**/

"He told the others to **hold on** to planks of wood or parts of the ship." (Acts 27:44)

"Wisdom is a life-giving tree, the source of happiness for all who **hold on** to her." (Proverbs 3:18)

Here's a fun reading activity if you have some time to prepare. Put students in pairs and give each pair a complete set of sentences from Appendix M that you have prepared in advance by printing and cutting apart along the dotted lines. Their job is to read through the sections and put the story back into a logical order.

Reading
5–10 minutes

Give them a reasonable deadline to finish—something that will push them but not stress them out. When time is up, ask for a volunteer to read his or her version of the text to the class. Discuss if the text was put together correctly. If not, the class can help make corrections.

Let's do speaking before pronunciation today and use one of the sentences from today's Scripture passage to review what the students have learned about linking words together from lessons 5, 11, and 12. Write this sentence on the board:

Speaking
5–7 minutes

- "The angel looked as bright as lightning, and his clothes were white as snow."

Ask students to predict which kinds of words will be stressed (nouns, verbs, adjectives, and adverbs) and which are unstressed (pronouns, helping verbs, conjunctions, prepositions, and articles). Underline the stressed words. When you are finished, your sentence should look something like this:

- "The <u>angel</u> <u>looked</u> as <u>bright</u> as <u>lightning</u>, and his <u>clothes</u> were <u>white</u> as <u>snow</u>."

Practice saying the sentence together, stressing the underlined words. Try clapping on each stressed word (with a little extra pause at the comma) so students can see that there is an equal space of time between each of the stressed words.

Ask the students to tell you if they see any of the following pronunciation patterns in the sentence:

1. Are there any silent letters?
   (*gh* in *bright* and *lightning*, *th* in *clothes*, *h* in *white*, *w* in *snow*)

2. Are there any words ending with *y* and followed by a vowel?
   (none, though "the angel" will have a *y* sound between the words to connect them; also see number 4)

3. Do you see *t* between two vowel sounds, where it would be pronounced as a "flap t"?
   (*bright as, white as*)

4. How would you pronounce *the* before the word *angel*?
   ("thee angel"—also using *y* to connect the two words: thee-y-angel)

5. Do you see any words ending with a consonant sound and the next word starts with a vowel sound?
   ("looked as"—there is a consonant *k* sound before the ending *t* sound, so the *t* keeps its pronunciation and is not changed to a "flap t.")

6. Are there any words that end with a consonant sound and the next word begins with the same consonant sound?
   (angellooked)

 Add their suggestions to the sentence. It might look something like this:

- Thee‿yangel‿look‿tas bri‿das litning, an‿dis cloz‿wer whi‿das sno.

Pronounce it slowly with exaggerated mouth movements so students can understand how the sounds are linked. Ask the students to repeat the sentence after you several times. You could also call on individual students who are confident in their pronunciation to say the sentence.

The Sounds of O

The five vowels of the English alphabet can make nineteen different sounds. The vowel *o* is no exception, and there are several examples in today's Scripture passage of the different sounds it can make.

Long *O*

Students should already be familiar with the long *o* sound. It is a diphthong, or "moving vowel." The mouth position changes as the sound is produced: *oh-oo*. Ask students to put a finger on each side of their mouths as they say long *o*. They should be able to feel that their mouth changes position while they say the sound. The sound needs a little time to produce, and that's why it's called a "long" vowel.

Below are the words with long *o* from today's Scripture passage. Pronounce them and have students repeat several times.

> **over, almost, rolled, stone, clothes, snow, though, know, don't, go, foll<u>o</u>wers**

Short *O*

Short o makes an *aah* sound and is, like its name implies, a "short" sound, taking only a moment to make the sound. Pronounce the following words from the Scripture passage and ask students to repeat several times after you.

> **on, strong, cross, God, body, f<u>o</u>llowers**

The *Oo* Sound

O can make an *oo* sound, sometimes considered one of the two long *u* sounds. It can be spelled *oo*, though we don't have any examples of this in today's Scripture passage. It is also a "long" sound, so encourage the students to take their time and concentrate on saying it correctly.

> **tomb, to, who, you** (not found in text: zoo, do, too, food, moon)

The *Euh* Sound

Sometimes words that are spelled with *oo* make an *euh* sound, as in *push*. These words typically end with *d* or *k*, but not always.

> **looked, shook, would** (not in text: book, cook, good, hood, could, should)

We are not considering spelling here. Many of these words just have to be memorized. As we reviewed in the speaking exercise, words can change their pronunciation in combination with other words in a sentence.

Other Sounds of *O*

O can make other sounds, including the short *u*, or *uh* as in *butter*. Pronounce these examples and ask students to repeat:

Teacher Tip

Digraph:

The word *digraph* means "two letters." A digraph is one sound spelled by two letters. *Sh* is an example of two letters that make one consonant sound. *Oo* is an example of two letters that make one vowel sound, as in *zoo*.

Diphthong

The word *diphthong* means "two sounds." A diphthong begins as one vowel sound and moves toward another. That is why these sounds can be called "moving vowels."

Long *a* and long *i* are also diphthongs. A common diphthong made with two letters is *ow* as in h*ow*. Because it is spelled with two letters, *ow* is also a digraph.

other, from, come

When combined with *r*, it becomes "r-controlled":

Lord, for, worshiped (pronounced "wershuhpt")

O can be combined with *w* to make the diphthong *ow* as in *how*:

down, now

In the irregular pronunciation of *women*, it can make a short *i* or *ih* sound. Contrast the pronunciations of *women* and *woman*.

women (wihmen)
woman (wuhmen)

Like all vowels, it can become a schwa in unstressed syllables:

(not in text: occur, concern)

Practice these words and sounds by writing them on the board as you say them. Choose a student to pronounce a word after you demonstrate the correct pronunciation. Then read today's Scripture passage in unison as a class.

Spelling
5–8 minutes

Dictate ten of the words with *o* that you discussed in the pronunciation exercise. Mix them up from the different sections. Have students compare answers in pairs to check their work.

Ask for a volunteer to tell you orally how their pair spelled a word. (You might need to review how to pronounce the letters of the alphabet.) Ask the rest of the class to raise their hands if they agree with that spelling. If the class is having trouble with any word, write it correctly on the board and practice pronouncing that word as a class.

Grammar
20 minutes

The Preposition/Conjunction/Adverb *As*

The word *as* has many jobs. Even though our focus in this series is on prepositions, it is much more common to see *as* used as an adverb or a conjunction. If you have beginners, only talk about *as* used as a preposition. More advanced learners may appreciate learning about the other uses of *as*.

1. First, we'll look at *as* used as a preposition.
2. Second, we'll look at its use as an adverb.
3. Finally, we'll look at *as* in its job as a conjunction.

We have examples of all three in our Scripture passage today.

1. The Preposition *As*

When *as* is used as a preposition, it describes someone or something by comparing it to someone or something else. Students will see this more in writing than in speaking because it sounds formal. Here's an example from the Scripture passage to write on the board:

- "His clothes were white **as** snow."

In this sample, the preposition *as* is followed by the noun *snow*, creating the prepositional phrase *as snow*. Erase the words "as snow." You are left with:

- His clothes were white.

Ask the students if they think this is a complete sentence (yes). Ask them if they think the sentence is more interesting with the added detail from the prepositional phrase.

Here are three more examples:

- "His brothers were jealous of him and sold him **as** a slave to be taken to Egypt." (Acts 7:9)

- "I have been with you **as** a servant." (Luke 22:27)

- "My Father has given me the right to rule **as** a king." (Luke 22:29)

These verses have the word *as* followed by a noun, so *as* is a preposition. These sentences would still be grammatically complete without the prepositional phrase, but the information in the prepositional phrases make the sentences more descriptive and interesting.

Explain how to construct a prepositional phrase with *as*. Write on the board:

- as + uncountable noun
- as + a/an/the + countable noun

Write these sentence starters on the board and ask for volunteers to orally suggest endings for each sentence by using a prepositional phrase beginning with *as*. Here are some suggestions:

- He is working as (a waiter / a bus driver / an engineer).
- I use that chair as (a desk / a clothes rack / a workbench).
- That is a picture of me as (a child / a teenager / a graduating senior).
- My brother's tie is blue as (the ocean / the sky / a robin's egg).

End the grammar exercise here if you have beginners.

2. The Conjunction *As*

As can also be a conjunction. This use is common and joins two clauses in the same sentence. Write these examples on the board:

1. "**As** Jesus was walking down a road, a man ran up to him." (Mark 10:17)

2. "Just **as** Jonah was a sign to the people of Nineveh, the Son of Man will be a sign to the people of today." (Luke 11:30)

Teacher Tip

The word *like* can sometimes substitute for the word *as* when it is used as a preposition or a conjunction. This is common in speaking because it is more casual. Currently, using *like* is also grammatically acceptable.

Conjunction:

"… just as I am" (1 Corinthians 16:10)

You could say, "… just like I am."

Preposition:

"God treated him as a sinner." (2 Corinthians 5:21)

You could say, "God treated him like a sinner."

Try substituting *like* for *as* in the sample sentences where *as* is used as a preposition. If *as* is being used as a conjunction, using *like* may or may not work.

3. "I have often wanted to gather your people, **as** a hen gathers her chicks under her wings." (Luke 13:34)

Ask students to notice that the clause beginning with *as* can appear at the beginning of a sentence or at the end of a sentence. When it is at the beginning, it will be joined to the rest of the sentence by a comma. If it appears at the end of a sentence, the comma may sometimes be omitted. Rewrite the first sentence so the *as* clause is at the end of the sentence.

- A man ran up to Jesus **as** he was walking down the road.

In this sentence, we don't need the comma. Ask students to help you reverse the order of sample sentences 2 and 3. (A comma is needed in both sentences.) Write them on the board.

- The Son of Man will be a sign to the people of today, just **as** Jonah was a sign to the people of Nineveh.

- **As** a hen gathers her chicks under her wings, I have often wanted to gather your people.

There is an example of the conjunction *as* in today's text. Ask students to look through their copy of the reading text and raise their hands when they see it. Wait until almost all of the students have raised their hands, then call on the first student who raised his or her hand to give the answer:

- "God has raised him to life, just **as** Jesus said he would."

For more practice, ask students to reverse the order of the clauses in this sentence:

- **As** Jesus said he would, God has raised him to life.

3. The Adverb *As*

When *as* is being used as an adverb, it will be followed by an adjective, an adverb, or a word such as *much* or *many*. It will usually appear in the format "as ... as." This use is common and is often used in informal speech as well as more formal writing. Here's an example from today's lesson to write on the board:

- "The angel looked **as** bright **as** lightning."

The first *as* (the adverb) is describing something by comparing it to something else. This *as* is followed by an adjective or an adverb. The second *as* is functioning as a preposition, followed by a noun. The entire phrase is an adverb, answering the question "how?" How did it look? It looked as bright as lightning.

Below are two more examples to write on the board. Ask students to identify the adjective or adverb that comes after the first *as*, the adverb. Then ask them to identify the noun that comes after the second *as*, the preposition. We'll practice more during the writing exercise today.

- "So be as wise as snakes and as innocent as doves." (Matthew 10:16)
- "The seed grows as big as a tree." (Luke 13:19)

Expressions with *As*

Here's another use of *as* found in today's Scripture passage:

- "The guards shook from fear and fell down, **as though** they were dead."

As though is an expression that means "in a way that suggests something else." In this sentence, as though is a conjunction that begins a clause that compares one thing to something else. This sentence compares the fact that the guards shook from fear and fell down with the statement that it looked as if they were dead.

Here's another example. Ask students what two things are being compared in this verse:

- "When you were baptized, it was **as though** you had put on Christ in the same way you put on new clothes." (Galatians 3:27)
  (comparing putting on Christ to putting on new clothes)

There are many other expressions that use *as*, and they all have the general meaning of comparison.

Have the students do another "finish the sentence" exercise, but this time each student will choose three of the following sentence starters and write their own sentence endings into their notebooks. Write these on the board:

1. The child was as _____ as _____.
2. That new car is as _____ as _____.
3. My job is as _____ as _____.
4. This rose is as _____ as _____.

Pair students to check sentences with each other. Offer each student a chance to come to the board and share a sentence with the class.

Teacher Tip

As though can describe an unreal or improbable situation, as in these examples. This requires the subjunctive mood—*were* and *had put*—in the *as though* clause.

The subjunctive is not used in English as much as it is in other languages, and many native English speakers use it incorrectly. If your students ask about it, tell them it's a topic for later, in an advanced-level class.

Writing
10–15 minutes

The Story of Easter

Lesson 19

Report of the Guard

While the women were on their way, some soldiers who had been guarding the tomb went into the city. They told the chief priests everything that had happened. So the chief priests met with the leaders and decided to bribe the soldiers with a lot of money. They said to the soldiers, "Tell everyone that Jesus' disciples came during the night and stole his body while you were asleep. If the governor hears about this, we will talk to him. You won't have anything to worry about." The soldiers took the money and did what they were told. The people of Judea still tell each other this story. (Matthew 28:11–15)

Introduce the Lesson
5–7 minutes

The guards in this passage were told by the religious leaders to start rumors. For this introduction, talk a bit with the students about how rumors get started and how damaging they can be.

- When you read something on the internet, do you ever stop and wonder if it is really true?
- Have you ever believed something that you found out later was not true?
- Have you ever heard something that was true, but you didn't believe it?

Listening Comprehension
10 minutes

Write these five multiple-choice comprehension questions on the board before you read to the class or print them out from Appendix N before class and pass them out. Students will write the answers in their notebooks or on the question paper as you read.

Read a second time so students can check their answers, then put them in pairs for a couple of minutes to compare their choices. Ask for volunteers to give the right answer and discuss any wrong answers. Read this short passage again so students can see where the answers appeared.

1. The soldiers who had been guarding the tomb
   a. left the city to hide because they were afraid.
   b. went into the city.
   c. told the women to return to their homes.

2. They told the chief priests
    a. they had finished their job and wanted to be paid.
    b. they had fallen asleep on the job.
    c. everything that had happened.

3. The chief priests met with the leaders and decided to
    a. bribe the soldiers with a lot of money.
    b. punish the soldiers for letting the disciples steal the body.
    c. find the disciples to discover the truth.

4. The chief priests told the soldiers
    a. to leave the city and never return.
    b. to say that Jesus' disciples came during the night and stole the body.
    c. they didn't believe their story of earthquakes and angels.

5. The soldiers
    a. refused the money because they would not lie.
    b. took the money and left for Rome.
    c. took the money and did what they were told.

Vocabulary
10–15 minutes

Today's vocabulary list contains two words that can be either a noun or a verb depending on how they are used in a sentence. You may need to take a little extra time to explain this.

The idiom "on (their) way" might also require a few more examples before students understand. Ask them to help you think of more examples of "on (their) way." See the notes about the word *asleep*.

1. on (their) way
(idiom)–in the process of going or coming (uses a possessive pronoun between the words)
/ɑːn ðər ˈweɪ/

"Jesus was **on his way** to Jerusalem." (Luke 13:22)

"I am **on my way** to you." (John 17:13)

2. guard
(In today's text it is a verb, but it can also be a noun.)–to protect property, places, or people
/gɑːrd/

"They sealed it tight and placed soldiers there to **guard** it." (Matthew 27:66)

"That night in the fields near Bethlehem some shepherds **were guarding** their sheep." (Luke 2:8)

3. bribe

(In today's text it is a verb, but it can also be a noun.)–to give someone money or something valuable to persuade them to do what you want, especially something dishonest
/**braɪb**/

"... those people who are brutal or full of meanness or who **bribe** others."
(Psalm 26:9–10)

"His decisions are always fair, and you cannot **bribe** him to change his mind."
(Deuteronomy 10:17)

4. asleep

(adjective)–to be sleeping
/ə ˈ**sliːp**/

"Jesus was sound **asleep.**" (Matthew 8:24)
(*Sound asleep* means "sleeping very deeply.")

"The groom was late arriving, and the young women became drowsy and fell **asleep.**" (Matthew 25:5)
(To *fall asleep* means "to go to sleep.")

5. each other

(pronoun)–both members of a two-person group when they do something to or for the other
/ˌiːtʃ ˈʌ ðər/

"He will lead children and parents to love **each other** more." (Malachi 4:6)

"Have salt among you and live at peace with **each other.**" (Mark 9:50)

For reading today, pass out the Scripture passage written on paper for students. Let them look it over and read silently to themselves for a minute or two.

Answer any questions about unfamiliar vocabulary, but don't spend an excessive amount of time. Read the passage out loud as the students read along.

Reading
5–10 minutes

Ay, Ey, Y Endings

Let's practice more with the letter *y*. *Y* is a common word ending. However, it can make different sounds depending on what letter precedes it.
For reference, here are the words from today's text that end with *y*. Write them on the board:

Pronunciation
20 minutes

way, city, they, every (thing), money, body, any (thing), worry, story

Ay Endings

Underline the word *way* as an example of a word that ends in *ay*. When a word ends with the spelling *ay*, the *ay* usually makes the long *a* sound. It is a common ending for many English words.

Write the following words on the board, pronounce them for the students, and ask them to repeat after you, both as a group and individually. See if they can suggest more words that end in *ay*. If they can't think of any, suggest *day, pray, pay,* and *lay*.

way (not in text: play, may, say)

Ey Endings

Underline *they* and *money* as examples from the Scripture passage of words that end in *ey*. The pronunciation of *ey* can be long *a* or long *e*. The long *e* sound is more common. There are some patterns, but not really any rules that would be easy for students to remember. It's easiest for students to just learn these words individually.

Write the following words on the board and practice them as you did the first group. Make sure students know the definitions. See if students can think of any more words ending in *ey* (e.g., *turkey, survey, hey, honey*).

they, money (not in text: key, obey, alley)

Consonant + Y Endings

When *y* at the end of a word is preceded by a consonant, it will almost always make the long *e* sound. Common exceptions are one-syllable words where *y* is the only vowel and makes the long *i* sound, like *cry* and *try*. Tell the students that if they see "consonant + *y*" at the end of a longer word and pronounce it as long *e*, they will almost always be right.

Underline the rest of the words from the story today and practice them as you did the first two groups. See if students can suggest more words that end with a "consonant + *y*" (e.g., *happy, party, empty, ready, twenty/thirty,* etc.).

city, every (thing), body, any (thing), worry, story

Erase all the words from the board and ask the students to get out a pencil and paper. Dictate any of the *ay, ey,* or "consonant + *y*" words you just practiced and ask the students to spell them correctly.

Have them exchange completed papers with the students next to them for checking. Ask for volunteers to come to the board and write one correct word. Check that the spelling is correct and let the students check their own work.

Remind the students that there is only one more lesson that will conclude the story of Easter. Ask them to come up with adjectives that describe how they feel about the story so far (e.g., *hope, fear, sadness, surprise, anger*). Write them on the board. Go around the room and let each student choose one or two adjectives and orally create a sentence about the Easter story and some of the characters in the story.

Ask them who they remember most from the story so far (e.g., Mary and the other Mary, the chief priests, Peter, the soldiers). Ask why that character was so memorable to them.

Ask if they remember what Jesus wanted the disciples to do at the end of lesson 18 (go to Galilee). If they don't remember, read the passage from lesson 18 to them again. See if they can predict what Jesus might say when he sees the disciples again. Tell them they will discover the answer in next week's lesson.

Speaking

5–7 minutes

The First Conditional

Teaching the conditional mood is generally done for upper-intermediate students. However, a quick understanding of the most common form of the conditional, the first conditional, will be useful for an advanced-beginner or lower-intermediate student, because it is common in daily conversation.

A conditional sentence consists of two clauses: the "if" clause and the resulting action in the other ("results") clause.

An Example from Today's Text

Tell students that the first conditional is used to talk about an event that is likely to happen in the future. This is the formula for making the first conditional. Write on the board:

If + present simple, will + base verb

Write on the board this example of the first conditional from our text today:

- "If the governor hears about this, we will talk to him."

In this sentence, the condition is whether or not the governor will hear about this. This information goes into the "if" clause. Underline the "if" clause.

- "<u>If the governor hears about this</u>, we will talk to him."

Circle the verb *hears* in the "if" clause.

- "<u>If the governor hears about this</u>, we will talk to him."

Ask students what tense this is. (present simple)

Now underline the "results" clause. This is where the likely consequences of the "if" clause are stated:

Grammar

15 minutes

Teacher Tip

There are four conditional forms: zero, first, second, and third. Below is a brief outline of the forms. Notice how the verb tenses change.

Zero Conditional

If you turn on the oven, it gets hot. (general fact)

First Conditional

If he studies, he will pass the exam. (likely future event)

Second Conditional

If he studied harder, he would pass the test. (unlikely future event because in reality he does not study hard)

Third Conditional

If he had studied harder, he would have passed the exam. (a past situation that did not happen)

- "If the governor hears about this, <u>we will talk to him</u>."

Ask students what tense the verb in the "results" clause is. (future simple) Circle the second verb.

- "If the governor hears about this, w̶e̶ ̶w̶i̶l̶l̶ ̶t̶a̶l̶k̶ ̶t̶o̶ ̶him."

More Examples

Below are more examples. Write them on the board one at a time. Ask students to identify the "if" clause with the verb in the present simple. Then ask them to identify the "results" clause with the verb in the future simple.

- "If you honor the Lord, his angel will protect you." (Psalm 34:7)

- "If you keep thinking about something, you will dream about it. If you talk too much, you will say the wrong thing." (Ecclesiastes 5:3)

Using Commas in the First Conditional

When the "if" clause comes first, a comma separates the two clauses.

- "If you return to God and turn from sin, all will go well for you." (Job 22:23)

The order of the clauses can be reversed.

- All will go well for you if you return to God and turn from sin.

You may or may not need to use a comma to separate the clauses when the "if" clause comes at the end. Tell your students that if they would make a significant pause when speaking, use a comma when writing.

Here is an example that uses a comma for emphasis when the "if" clause comes last:

- "Everything you ask for in prayer will be yours, if you only have faith." (Mark 11:24)

A comma is needed if you reverse the clauses and put the "if" clause at the beginning:

- If you only have faith, everything you ask for in prayer will be yours.

Here's another example:

- "If you obey the Lord, he will watch over you and answer your prayers." (Psalm 34:15)

With this example, you don't need a comma when you put the "if" clause last, because you wouldn't pause when speaking:

- The Lord will watch over you and answer your prayers if you obey him.

The Story of Easter

If this is new to your students, stop here and proceed to the writing exercise. If you have a mixed group, put your beginners in a small group or groups to work on the writing exercise together while you continue with this grammar lesson for your more advanced students.

Questions in the First Conditional

Either clause can come first in a first conditional question. However, the only clause that changes to become a question is the "results" clause. Below are some questions in the first conditional. Write them on the board.

- "What will you gain, if you own the whole world but destroy yourself or waste your life?" (Luke 9:25)
- "What will a woman do if she has ten silver coins and loses one of them?" (Luke 15:8)

Ask the students to identify the verbs. Have them identify the "if" clause by telling you where the verb in the present tense is. Let them identify the "results" clause by telling you where the verb in the future tense is.

Notice that the question is formed in the clause with the future simple verb. Put the subject between the "will" and the base verb.

Ask them to reverse the order of the clauses in each question. The clause with the future simple verb changes into a question whether it is first or second.

Ask if the following questions need a comma. (They do, because we are now putting the "if" clause first.)

- If you own the whole world but destroy yourself or waste your life, what will you gain?
- If a woman has ten silver coins and loses one of them, what will she do?

Negative Sentences in the First Conditional

We've seen that only the "results" clause can be made into a question in the first conditional. However, either or both clauses can be made negative by adding the appropriate negative helping verbs after the subject. Write this sentence on the board:

- If Sara calls, I'll go to the grocery store.

Ask students to help you make each clause negative and discuss the new meaning of each sentence. Practice with a second sentence if you have time. Let the students suggest a sentence to change.

- If Sara calls, I won't go to the grocery store.
- If Sara doesn't call, I'll go to the grocery store.
- If Sara doesn't call, I won't go to the grocery store.

Practice the first conditional with this writing exercise. Get enough slips of paper for everyone in the class to have one. Write an "if" clause on each one. Here are some ideas:

- If it rains,
- If I study,
- If I have enough money,
- If she calls,
- If the train is late,
- If they don't leave soon,
- If I see him,
- If I win the lottery,
- If I am free,
- If we practice hard,
- If I stay home,

Give one slip to each student. Have students circulate around the room with their slips of paper and talk with one another. Ask them to find out what the other person has on their slip of paper, then orally finish the other person's sentence. (They can write the sentences in their notebooks if they choose.)

When each student has had a chance to compare sentence starters with three or four other students, have them all return to their seats and share with the class some of the sentences they created. As time permits, write as many of them as possible on the board and check for correct grammar.

ᴛʜᴇ Story of Easter

Lesson 20

What Jesus' Followers Must Do

Jesus' eleven disciples went to a mountain in Galilee, where Jesus had told them to meet him. They saw him and worshiped him, but some of them doubted.

Jesus came to them and said:

I have been given all authority in heaven and on earth! Go to the people of all nations and make them my disciples. Baptize them in the name of the Father, the Son, and the Holy Spirit, and teach them to do everything I have told you. I will be with you always, even until the end of the world. (Matthew 28:16–20)

Since this is the last lesson in this series about the story of Easter, we are going to go a little off-script and review some of the things students have studied in this course. First, introduce the Scripture passage for today's lesson by asking either or both of the following questions, or make up a question of your own.

Introduce the Lesson
5–7 minutes

- Why do you think people might doubt (not believe) something they know in their hearts is true?
- How would you feel if your boss told you to do something but didn't give you the instructions or the materials and tools to do it?

Write the following comprehension questions on the board before you read the Scripture passage to the class. Ask the students to listen for the answers as you read the text to them. When you have finished reading, go through the questions and see if the students heard the answers. If they need help, read the passage again.

Listening Comprehension
10 minutes

- How many disciples went to Galilee? (eleven)
- What did they do after they saw Jesus? (worshiped him)
- What would the people of all nations be made? (Jesus' disciples)
- In the name of the Father, the Son, and the Holy Spirit, what would the new disciples be? (baptized)
- How long will Jesus be with us? (always)

Reading
5–10 minutes

Today we're going to do reading before we do vocabulary. Give each student a copy of the Scripture passage written on paper. Let them look it over for a few minutes. Then read it out loud to them as they read along.

Ask them if they have any questions about any of the words in the text. We won't be learning any new vocabulary today, so this is their chance to ask you what a word means. If you have time and your students seem confident, go around the room several times and ask them to take turns reading out loud, one sentence at a time.

Vocabulary/ Spelling
10–15 minutes

Today's text is short and contains vocabulary the students probably already know. Check with them quickly to be sure they understand the meaning of each word in the passage. Students will do a worksheet to review some of the vocabulary they have learned in this book.

Make a copy of the vocabulary review crossword puzzle from Appendix O for each student. Use the version with a word bank for beginners; use the version without a word bank for your more advanced students. Give them a time limit of five minutes or so, depending on the ability of your students. Put them in small groups to compare answers for another three minutes. Call on one member from each group to give you the answer for every blank.

Pronunciation
15 minutes

Review of Word Linking

In this course, we talked about linking words together. We've done a few practice sentences, so let's do one more.

Word Stress Practice

See if the students can help you figure out which words in the following sentence would be stressed, and which would be unstressed.

- "I will be with you always, even until the end of the world."

Answer:
- I will be **with** you **always, even** until the **end** of the **world.**

Ask for volunteers to tell you the kinds of words that are stressed and unstressed.

Answer:
Stressed words are:
- nouns (end, world)
- verbs (in this sentence, since we are stressing the word *with*, we probably won't stress the verb *be*)
- adjectives
- adverbs (always, even)

Unstressed words are:
- helping verbs (will)
- prepositions (until, of, with)
  Note: In this sentence, the preposition *with* is stressed, because it adds meaning to the sentence and is an important word: God is **with** us.
- articles (the)
- pronouns (I, you)
- conjunctions

Word stress also depends on the meaning of the sentence and the speaker's intention. That's why, in this example, the preposition *with* is stressed instead of the verb *be*. *With* carries a lot of meaning in this sentence.

Help students to hear the rhythm of the spoken sentence by clapping at every stressed word. Note the similar interval of time between stressed words, including the pause indicated by the comma. Practice as a group reading the sentence out loud with the stressed words, then ask for volunteers to read it by themselves.

Word Linking Practice

Now let's link some of these words together. Ask students for their input and write their ideas into the sentence on the board. Here's our sentence with linked sounds:

- I will be with‿yoo‿w–alwayz, evə n‿until thee‿y–en d‿əv th'world.

1. Link end consonants to the first letter of the next word if it is a vowel (lesson 5)

2. Insert extra *w* or *y* sound if one word ends with a vowel sound and the next word begins with a vowel sound (lesson 12)

3. Note the schwa sound in the second syllable of *even*. In reduced form, *of* says "əv" (lesson 2)

4. Before a vowel, *the* says "thee," with a *y* sound or a *w* sound connecting the two vowels (lesson 12)

5. *S* is pronounced *z* in *always* (lesson 7)

English is not a phonetic language. (One letter can make several different sounds.) That's one reason it has a well-deserved reputation for being hard to pronounce. Dissecting a sentence in this way gives students more confidence in their pronunciation. In my experience, many students enjoy this kind of exercise. If you have time, and your students want to, do the same with another sentence from today's Scripture passage, or let the students make up a sentence to dissect in this way.

Today we'll play Twenty Questions, a fun, classic game for ESL students. You may choose to do this at the end of today's lesson, after the final quiz, if you wish.

Have the students sit in a circle. Go over the rules of the game if students have never played before. Tell them you will think of a noun in one of three categories: a person, a place, or a thing. Students will take turns asking you one question that can be answered with a yes or a no.

They have twenty questions to figure out what noun you are thinking of. The student who guesses correctly during his turn after asking a question gets to choose the next noun.

Go around the circle asking questions. If a student guesses the answer, that student comes to the middle of the circle and chooses a noun for the others to guess. Questions begin with the student who would have asked the next question.

Play a sample game with you thinking of the first noun:

You: I'm thinking of a noun.
Student 1: Is it a person?

You: No.
Student 2: Is it a thing?

You: Yes.
Student 3: Is it bigger than my notebook?

You: Yes.
Student 4: Is it made of metal?

You: No.
Student 5: Is it made of wood?

You: Yes.
Student 6: Is it a pencil?

You: No, it isn't a pencil.
Student 7: Is it in this room?

You: Yes.
Student 8: Is it a chair?

You: No.
Student 9: Is it a table?

You: Yes.

Student 9 stands in the middle of the circle and chooses the next noun. Student 10 asks the first question.

Before the game, you can write various nouns on the board, such as *wood, metal, glass,* or a person or place. If your noun is a person, stick with categories like dentist, actor, politician, or bus driver, not names of actual people.

Play as long as you have time or as long as student interest holds. Once your students learn this game, it can become a classroom staple for those times when you need easy speaking practice or have some extra time to fill at the beginning of class while waiting for students to arrive.

Final Grammar Quiz

Grammar/ Writing

25–30 minutes

Provide your students with another opportunity to prove their knowledge by giving them a quiz covering the prepositions we have learned in this course. Students expect a test, and it can encourage them by showing a concrete indication of how much they have learned during the course.

You'll find the printable test in Appendix P. Give your students twenty minutes to finish. If you have a class with multiple levels, lower-level students can do the first half of the questions in each section while higher-level students can do all of the questions in the same amount of time.

When everyone is finished, check the answers as a class. Go around the room and ask each student to answer one question. Before you confirm whether the answer is correct or incorrect, ask the entire class if anyone had a different answer. If other answers are mentioned, discuss how the students arrived at their answers before you supply the correct one.

Ask the next student to provide the answer for question 2 and proceed in this way through the test. And when you've finished grading the test, congratulate them on a job well done!

You might want to schedule another time for your class to get together and have a party—more opportunities to form friendships, talk about the Bible, and practice English in a casual setting. One idea would be to have everyone bring a traditional dish from their family or heritage and have a meal together. Play Twenty Questions again, or try another game. A Pictionary-type game is also a fun option.

The Story of Easter

Appendix A

Prepositions of Location: *In*, *On*, and *At*

_____

Add the correct preposition to each of the following sentences. Some sentences may have more than one correct answer.

1. He's playing tennis _____ the park.

2. Where's Rebecca? She's _____ work.

3. The plate is _____ the table.

4. There are books _____ the box.

5. Please put the silverware _____ the drawer.

6. There are three candles _____ the shelf.

7. Lucy was standing _____ the bus stop.

8. I read the story _____ the magazine.

9. I'll meet you _____ the restaurant.

10. I read that article _____ the internet.

Appendix A–Answers

1. He's playing tennis _at_ the park.
    (Possibly *in*, though that doesn't specify which tennis court, the one in the park.)

2. Where's Rebecca? She's _at_ work.

3. The plate is _on_ the table.

4. There are books _in_ the box.

5. Please put the silverware _in_ the drawer.

6. There are three candles _on_ the shelf.

7. Lucy was standing _at_ the bus stop.

8. I read the story _in_ the magazine.

9. I'll meet you _at_ the restaurant.

10. I read that article _on_ the internet.

THE Story of Easter

Appendix B

Prepositions of Time: *In*, *On*, *At*, and *During*

Add the correct preposition to each of the following sentences. There may be more than one correct answer to some sentences.

1. It rains a lot _____ the spring.

2. George Washington was born _____ February 22, 1732.

3. We usually have friends over _____ the weekend.

4. Our family has great conversations _____ dinner.

5. I have a job interview _____ 10:00.

6. They got married _____ June.

7. We clapped a lot _____ the show.

8. Birds fly south _____ the winter.

9. I always get up _____ 7:00.

10. _____ the 19th century, many immigrants came to America.

Appendix B—Answers

1. It rains a lot _in_ the spring.
   (possibly *during*)

2. George Washington was born _on_ February 22, 1732.

3. We usually have friends over _on_ the weekend.
   (British English *at*)

4. Our family has great conversations _during_ dinner.
   (possibly *at*)

5. I have a job interview _at_ 10:00.

6. They got married _in_ June.
   (possibly *during*, but *in* is better for a one-time event like this)

7. We clapped a lot _during_ the show.

8. Birds fly south _in_ the winter.

9. I always get up _at_ 7:00.

10. _During_ the 19th century, many immigrants came to America.
    (also *in*)

THE Story of Easter

Appendix C

Subject and Object Pronouns

Choose the correct pronoun for each blank. The verb in the sentence or clause is in bold to help you notice whether the blank is before or after the verb. Watch for compound sentences with more than one clause. Not all of the pronouns in the box will be used. Some sentences can have more than one correct answer.

Subject pronouns (before the verb): *I, you, he, she, it, we, they*

Object pronouns (after the verb): *me, you, him, her, it, us, them*

1. "He healed our diseases and **made** _____ well." (Matthew 8:17)

2. "This was Jesus' first miracle, and he **did** _____ in the village of Cana in Galilee." (John 2:11)

3. "When he was raised from death, his disciples remembered what (a)_____ **had told** them. Then (b) _____ **believed** the Scriptures and the words of Jesus." (John 2:22)

4. "Nathanael said, 'Rabbi, _____ **are** the Son of God and the King of Israel!" (John 1:49)

5. "The man's parents answered, '_____ **are** certain that he is our son.'" (John 9:20)

6. "Everyone calls me a nobody, but _____ **remember** your laws." (Psalm 119:141)

7. "As soon as Mary said this, _____ **turned around** and saw Jesus standing there." (John 20:14)

8. "Mary has chosen what is best, and it **will** not **be** taken away from _____." (Luke 10:42)

Appendix C–Answers

1. "He healed our diseases and made _us_ well." (Matthew 8:17)
   (Use *us* because of *our* in the first part of the sentence.)

2. "This was Jesus' first miracle, and he did _it_ in the village of Cana in Galilee." (John 2:11)

3. "When he was raised from death, his disciples remembered what (a) _he_ had told them. Then (b) _they_ believed the Scriptures and the words of Jesus." (John 2:22)

4. "Nathanael said, 'Rabbi, _you_ are the Son of God and the King of Israel!'" (John 1:49)

5. "The man's parents answered, '_We_ are certain that he is our son.'" (John 9:20)
   (Use *we* because we are talking about the plural, *parents*.)

6. "Everyone calls me a nobody, but _I_ remember your laws." (Psalm 119:141)
   (*I* is correct, because the first clause uses *me*. Notice also that the verb *remember* does not have the third person singular *s* on the end, so the answer would not be *he* or *she*.)

7. "As soon as Mary said this, _she_ turned around and saw Jesus standing there." (John 20:14)
   (*She* is correct because it refers to Mary.)

8. "Mary has chosen what is best, and it will not be taken away from _her_." (Luke 10:42)
   (*Her* is correct because the first clause refers to Mary.)

The Story of Easter

Appendix D

Lesson 9: Listening Comprehension

Fill in the blanks in the following story with the word you hear. If it is a verb, make sure it matches the subject of the sentence.

After Jesus had been arrested, he was led off to the house of Caiaphas the high priest. The nation's leaders and the teachers of the Law of Moses were meeting there. But Peter followed along at a distance and came to the (1) _____ of the high priest's palace. He went in and sat down with the guards to see what was going to happen.

The chief priests and the whole council wanted to put Jesus to death. So they tried to find some people who would tell lies about him in court. But they could not find any, (2)_____ _____ many did come and tell lies.

(3)_____, two men came forward and said, "This man claimed he could (4)_____ _____ God's temple and build it again in three days."

The high priest stood up and asked Jesus, "Why don't you say something in your own defense? Don't you hear the charges they are making against you?" But Jesus did not answer. So the high priest said, "With the living God looking on, you must tell the (5)_____. Are you the Messiah, the Son of God?"

"That is what you say!" Jesus answered. "But I tell all of you, 'Soon you will see the Son of Man sitting at the right side of God All-Powerful and coming on the clouds of heaven.'"

The high priest then tore his robe and said, "This man claims to be God! We don't (6)_____ any more witnesses! You have heard what he said. What do you think?"

They answered, "He is guilty and (7)_____ to die!" Then they spit in his face and hit him with their fists. Others slapped him and said, "You think you are the Messiah! So tell us who hit you!" (Matthew 26:57–68)

Appendix D—Answers

After Jesus had been arrested, he was led off to the house of Caiaphas the high priest. The nation's leaders and the teachers of the Law of Moses were meeting there. But Peter followed along at a distance and came to the (1) <u>courtyard</u> of the high priest's palace. He went in and sat down with the guards to see what was going to happen.

The chief priests and the whole council wanted to put Jesus to death. So they tried to find some people who would tell lies about him in court. But they could not find any, (2) <u>even though</u> many did come and tell lies.

(3) <u>At last</u>, two men came forward and said, "This man claimed he could (4) <u>tear down</u> God's temple and build it again in three days."

The high priest stood up and asked Jesus, "Why don't you say something in your own defense? Don't you hear the charges they are making against you?" But Jesus did not answer. So the high priest said, "With the living God looking on, you must tell the (5) <u>truth</u>. Are you the Messiah, the Son of God?"

"That is what you say!" Jesus answered. "But I tell all of you, 'Soon you will see the Son of Man sitting at the right side of God All-Powerful and coming on the clouds of heaven.'"

The high priest then tore his robe and said, "This man claims to be God! We don't (6) <u>need</u> any more witnesses! You have heard what he said. What do you think?"

They answered, "He is guilty and (7) <u>deserves</u> to die!" Then they spit in his face and hit him with their fists. Others slapped him and said, "You think you are the Messiah! So tell us who hit you!" (Matthew 26:57–68)

The Story of Easter

Appendix E

Lesson 10: Speaking Roleplay

Narrator: While Peter was sitting out in the courtyard, a servant girl came up to him.

Servant Girl 1: You were with Jesus from Galilee.

Peter: That isn't so! I don't know what you are talking about!

Narrator: When Peter had gone out to the gate, another servant girl saw him.

Servant Girl 2: This man was with Jesus from Nazareth.

Narrator: Again Peter denied it, and this time he swore.

Peter: I don't even know that man!

Narrator: A little while later some people standing there walked over to Peter.

Group leader: We know you are one of them. We can tell it because you talk like someone from Galilee.

Narrator: Peter began to curse and swear.

Peter: I don't know that man!

Narrator: Right then a rooster crowed, and Peter remembered that Jesus had said,

Jesus: Before a rooster crows, you will say three times you don't know me.

Narrator: Then Peter went out and cried bitterly.

The Story of Easter

Appendix F

Lesson 11: Spelling

Circle the ten words from today's Bible passage that are spelled incorrectly.

Early the next morning all the chief priests and the nation's leaders met and decided that Jesus should be put to death. They tid him up and led him away to Pilate the governor.

Judas had betrayed Jesus, but when he learned that Jesus had been sentenced to death, he was sory for what he had done. He returned the 30 silver coins to the chief priests and leaders and said, "I have sinned by betraying a man who has never done anything wrong."

"So wat? That's your problem," they replied. Judas through the money into the temple and then went out and hanged himself.

The chief priests piked up the monee and said, "This money was paid to have a man killed. We can't put it in the temple treasury." Then they had a meeting and decided to by a field that bulonged to someone who made clay pets. They wanted to use it as a graveyard for foreigners. This is why people still call that place "Field of Blood."

So the werds of the prophet Jeremiah came true,

"They took the thirty silver coins,
the price of a person among the people of Israel.
They paid it for a potter's field,
as the Lord had commanded me." (Matthew 27:1–10)

Appendix F—Answers

Early the next morning all the chief priests and the nation's leaders met and decided that Jesus should be put to death. They **tied** him up and led him away to Pilate the governor.

Judas had betrayed Jesus, but when he learned that Jesus had been sentenced to death, he was **sorry** for what he had done. He returned the 30 silver coins to the chief priests and leaders and said, "I have sinned by betraying a man who has never done anything wrong."

"So **what?** That's your problem," they replied. Judas **threw** the money into the temple and then went out and hanged himself.

The chief priests **picked** up the **money** and said, "This money was paid to have a man killed. We can't put it in the temple treasury." Then they had a meeting and decided to **buy** a field that **belonged** to someone who made clay **pots.** They wanted to use it as a graveyard for foreigners. This is why people still call that place "Field of Blood."

So the **words** of the prophet Jeremiah came true,

> "They took the thirty silver coins,
>
> the price of a person among the people of Israel.
>
> They paid it for a potter's field,
>
> as the Lord had commanded me." (Matthew 27:1–10)

THE Story of Easter

Appendix G

Preposition: *Against*

For the following sentences with *against*, identify the object of the preposition: who or what is being opposed or disagreed with. Then identify the subject: who is doing the opposing. The first one is done for you.

Sample: "My friend turned against me and broke his promise." (Psalm 55:20)

> **Against who or what:** me
> **Who is opposing or disagreeing:** my friend

1. Abraham Lincoln ran against George B. McClellan for president in 1864.
   Against who or what:
   Who is opposing or disagreeing:

2. Some stores can't compete against Amazon.
   Against who or what:
   Who is opposing or disagreeing:

3. My coworkers seem to be working against me.
   Against who or what:
   Who is opposing or disagreeing:

4. I'm not against progress; I just like my old phone better.
   Against who or what:
   Who is opposing or disagreeing:

5. "Who will stand up for me against those cruel people?" (Psalm 94:16)
   Against who or what:
   Who is opposing or disagreeing:

Appendix G—Answers

1. Abraham Lincoln ran against George B. McClellan for president in 1864.
   Against who or what: George B. McClellan
   Who is opposing or disagreeing: Abraham Lincoln

2. Some stores can't compete against Amazon.
   Against who or what: Amazon
   Who is opposing or disagreeing: some stores

3. My coworkers seem to be working against me.
   Against who or what: me
   Who is opposing or disagreeing: my coworkers

4. I'm not against progress; I just like my old phone better.
   Against who or what: progress
   Who is opposing or disagreeing: I

5. "Who will stand up for me against those cruel people?" (Psalm 94:16)
   Against who or what: those cruel people
   Who is opposing or disagreeing: whoever will be against the cruel people

The Story of Easter

Appendix H

Minimal Pairs Bingo with Short *I* and Long *E*

To play Bingo, each student gets a card and enough "markers" (paper clips, seeds, pennies, etc.) to cover each square on their card. Don't duplicate cards if you have more than twelve students, because each student card needs to be unique. If you need more cards, you can create your own online at myfreebingocards.com. Print two caller's cards and cut one into small squares with one word on each square. Fold the squares and put them into a hat.

You should be the first caller.

The caller chooses a square of paper at random from the hat and pronounces the word for the students. Any students who think they have that word on their cards should put a marker on it. The caller puts a check next to that word on his or her card.

The space in the middle of a student card is free; they can put a marker on that at any time. No student will have all the words on his or her card because there are thirty-five words and only twenty-four spaces on a student card.

To win the game, a student must have five markers in a row up, down, or diagonally. When a student has five in a row, they shout, "Bingo!" The caller checks the student's card against the caller's card to be sure all the words were actually called. If the student has made a mistake, the game continues until there is a winner. The winner gets to call the next game.

This is where it gets even more fun. The winner works hard to pronounce the minimal pair words correctly so the rest of the class can mark the correct word.

Play continues until each student has had an opportunity to be the caller, or until you run out of time. You can have a vocabulary lesson before you play if students do not know all the words on the caller's card.

Create your own Bingo games with other minimal pairs to practice pronunciation.

Bingo Caller's Card

ship	pitch	hit	he'll	his	seek	peach
peel	rich	sheep	will	heat	pill	he's
been	green	fit	reach	ill	we'll	grin
seat	mill	bean	still	feet	sit	eel
hill	eat	sick	meal	gym	steel	it

Bingo Student Card 1

reach	he's	heat	still	rich
will	green	sick	gym	peach
pill	it	FREE SPACE	eat	been
fit	eel	hit	he'll	mill
hill	pitch	feet	bean	sheep

Bingo Student Card 2

eel	meal	we'll	seat	hill
seek	rich	steel	been	peel
sick	peach	FREE SPACE	his	still
green	will	sheep	ill	ship
mill	reach	hit	feet	pitch

Bingo Student Card 4

bean	pitch	pill	seek	sick
been	green	we'll	sit	meal
fit	pill	FREE SPACE	seat	we'll
pitch	eat	his	rich	green
bean	it	grin	mill	been

Bingo Student Card 3

been	ship	pitch	green	peel
bean	we'll	steel	gym	reach
hit	sick	FREE SPACE	feet	it
sit	ill	sheep	he's	peach
seek	fit	hill	eat	mill

fit	hit	hill	pitch	gym
rich	meal	seat	been	he's
peach	bean	FREE SPACE	pill	sit
eat	ship	sheep	eel	reach
seek	feet	steel	we'll	mill

heat	ill	seat	gym	still
hill	eat	ship	steel	mill
it	green	FREE SPACE	his	peach
heat	ill	seat	gym	still
meal	sheep	we'll	bean	hit

Bingo Student Card 7

gym	he'll	feet	we'll	reach
steel	his	fit	mill	still
meal	green	FREE SPACE	been	will
seat	sheep	heat	hit	it
sick	seek	hill	peel	sit

Bingo Student Card 8

his	hill	green	he's	seat
hit	been	meal	heat	fit
seek	sit	FREE SPACE	grin	peach
we'll	it	still	sick	ship
rich	ill	peel	eel	reach

Bingo Student Card 9

pitch	mill	we'll	still	hill
sit	sheep	he's	his	green
heat	been	FREE SPACE	pill	fit
ship	reach	steel	rich	peach
eat	he'll	hit	grin	it

Bingo Student Card 10

mill	seat	bean	sheep	pitch
ship	his	sick	eat	gym
he'll	meal	FREE SPACE	fit	will
it	he's	grin	hill	been
rich	we'll	hit	steel	green

Bingo Student Card 11

heat	been	eel	ship	he'll
mill	gym	he's	will	sheep
meal	peel	FREE SPACE	we'll	green
sick	seek	still	reach	fit
seat	it	steel	his	peach

Bingo Student Card 12

rich	reach	meal	peel	it
sick	grin	peach	heat	ill
pill	eat	FREE SPACE	will	sit
ship	gym	hill	steel	his
mill	been	fit	we'll	hit

THE Story of Easter

Appendix I

Prepositions: *From* and *Of*

_____

Choose the correct preposition for each blank. Be prepared to explain the answer you chose. Remember that *from* has to do with origins and *of* has to do with possession.

1. "He said, 'I wish I had a drink _____ the well by the gate at Bethlehem.'" (2 Samuel 23:15)

2. "Rescue the weak and homeless (a) _____ the powerful hands (b) _____ heartless people." (Psalm 82:4)

3. "Each time we pray for you, we thank God, the Father _____ our Lord Jesus Christ." (Colossians 1:3)

4. "Don't all those who are speaking come _____ Galilee?" (Acts 2:7)

5. "Then Isaiah told Hezekiah, 'I have a message for you _____ the Lord.'" (2 Kings 20:16)

6. "Yes, Lord!" she replied. "I believe you are the Christ, the Son _____ God." (John 11:27)

7. "He went back inside and asked Jesus, 'Where are you _____?'" (John 19:9)

8. "When Simon Peter got there, he went into the tomb and saw the strips ___ cloth." (John 20:6)

9. "When you are far _____ home, you feel like a bird without a nest." (Proverbs 27:8)

10. "God loved the people _____ this world so much that he gave his only Son." (John 3:16)

Appendix I—Answers

1. "He said, 'I wish I had a drink _from_ the well by the gate at Bethlehem.'" (2 Samuel 23:15)

2. "Rescue the weak and homeless (a) _from_ the powerful hands (b) _of_ heartless people." (Psalm 82:4)

3. "Each time we pray for you, we thank God, the Father _of_ our Lord Jesus Christ." (Colossians 1:3)

4. "Don't all those who are speaking come _from_ Galilee?" (Acts 2:7)

5. "Then Isaiah told Hezekiah, 'I have message for you _from_ the Lord.'" (2 Kings 20:16)

6. "Yes, Lord!" she replied. "I believe you are the Christ, the Son _of_ God." (John 11:27)

7. "He went back inside and asked Jesus, 'Where are you _from_?'" (John 19:9)

8. "When Simon Peter got there, he went into the tomb and saw the strips _of_ cloth." (John 20:6)

9. "When you are far _from_ home, you feel like a bird without a nest." (Proverbs 27:8)

10. "God loved the people _of_ this world so much that he gave his only Son." (John 3:16) (_From_ is also possible here, though the meaning would be slightly different.)

The Story of Easter

Appendix J

Reflexive Pronouns

Choose the correct reflexive pronoun from the word bank to finish each sentence. You may not use them all, and you will use some of the words more than once.

> **Word Bank**
>
> myself   yourself   himself   herself   itself   ourselves   yourselves   themselves

1. "They replied, 'Why do we need more witnesses? He said it _____!'" (Luke 22:71)

2. "Don't worry about tomorrow. It will take care of _____. You have enough to worry about today." (Matthew 6:34)

3. "They said to (a) _____, 'Someday he will own this vineyard. Let's kill him! That way we can have it all for (b) _____.'" (Mark 12:7)

4. "Respect your father and mother. And love others as much as you love _____." (Matthew 19:19)

5. "I always try to please others instead of _____, in the hope that many of them will be saved." (1 Corinthians 10:33)

6. "Some people want money so much they have given up their faith and caused _____ a lot of pain." (1 Timothy 6:10)

7. "All of you have seen these things for _____. So you have no excuse." (Job 27:12)

8. "It isn't because I don't love you. God _____ knows how much I do love you." (2 Corinthians 11:11)

9. "We arrived in Rome, and Paul was allowed to live in a house by _____ with a soldier to guard him." (Acts 28:16)

10. "Mighty armies alone cannot win wars for a king; great strength by _____ cannot keep a soldier safe." (Psalm 33:16)

Appendix J–Answers

1. "They replied, 'Why do we need more witnesses? He said it _himself_!'" (Luke 22:71)

2. "Don't worry about tomorrow. It will take care of _itself_. You have enough to worry about today." (Matthew 6:34)

3. "They said to (a) _themselves_, 'Someday he will own this vineyard. Let's kill him! That way we can have it all for (b) _ourselves_.'" (Mark 12:7)

4. "Respect your father and mother. And love others as much as you love _yourself_." (Matthew 19:19).
   (_Yourselves_ would also work grammatically.)

5. "I always try to please others instead of _myself_, in the hope that many of them will be saved." (1 Corinthians 10:33)

6. "Some people want money so much they have given up their faith and caused _themselves_ a lot of pain." (1 Timothy 6:10)

7. "All of you have seen these things for _yourselves_. So you have no excuse." (Job 27:12)

8. "It isn't because I don't love you. God _himself_ knows how much I do love you." (2 Corinthians 11:11)

9. "We arrived in Rome, and Paul was allowed to live in a house by _himself_ with a soldier to guard him." (Acts 28:16)

10. "Mighty armies alone cannot win wars for a king; great strength by _itself_ cannot keep a soldier safe." (Psalm 33:16)

THE Story of Easter

Appendix K

Irregular Past Participles

Below is a short list of some common English verbs with their irregular past participle forms. Try a review in the form of a game as described in lesson 17.

Base Verb	Irregular Past Participle	Base Verb	Irregular Past Participle
come	come	give	given
speak	spoken	tell	told
do	done	run	run
sing	sung	buy	bought
eat	eaten	make	made
bring	brought	send	sent
take	taken	write	written
have	had	teach	taught
find	found	throw	thrown
get	gotten	drive	driven
sell	sold	begin	begun
go	gone	forget	forgotten
leave	left	choose	chosen
be	been	feel	felt
meet	met	drink	drunk
pay	paid	grow	grown
see	seen	build	built
wear	worn	break	broken

Appendix L – Passive Tense Board Game

Instructions: Roll one die and move that number of spaces on the board. Orally finish the sentence with the passive form of the verb in parentheses (a form of the verb *be* + the past participle of the verb). You can use any verb tense you like as long as it makes sense in the sentence. If the participle is irregular, it is on the list in Appendix K. If you answer correctly, you can stay on that space. If you miss the answer, return to the square you were on and try again on your next turn.

Start Here	English ___ here. (speak)	The telephone ___ in 1876. (invent)	The sheep ___ all night long. (watch)	I ___ to leave my shoes on the mat. (tell)	The church office ___ every Friday. (clean)
A lot of cars ___ each week at that shop. (repair)	The new building ___ last year. (design)	My keys ___ on the kitchen table. (leave)	A backpack ___ in the school cafeteria. (find)	New projects ___ every week in that class. (turn in)	Cell phones ___ every day. (use)
The children ___ not to play there. (ask)	Jesus ___ by John. (baptize)	A lot of classic cars ___ to that car show. (bring)	I ___ the good news yesterday. (give)	Very expensive shoes ___ at that store. (sell)	That national park ___ by a lot of people. (love)
The flowers ___ in the front garden. (plant)	A lot of pizza ___ every day at that cafe. (serve)	The text message ___ two days ago. (send)	The package ___ before noon. (deliver)	Donated books ___ at the library weekly. (receive)	Songs of praise ___ to God. (sing)
Two of every kind of animal ___ on the Ark. (take)	All the houses ___ white. (paint)	This car ___ last year. (buy)	The temple ___ by King Solomon. (build)	The cooking class ___ by Mrs. Rosso. (teach)	**Finished** Well Done!

Appendix L–Answers

There are several possible answers to each sentence since students can choose a verb tense. For an answer to be correct, it should contain a form of the verb *be* + the past participle of the verb in parentheses. Just be sure the sentence makes sense grammatically.

English _____ here. (is/was/will be spoken)

The telephone _____ in 1876. (was invented)

The sheep _____ all night long. (are/were/will be watched)

I _____ to leave my shoes on the mat. (was told)

The church office _____ every Friday. (is/was/will be cleaned)

A lot of cars _____ each week at that shop. (are/were/will be repaired)

The new building _____ last year. (was designed)

My keys _____ on the kitchen table. (were left)

A backpack _____ in the school cafeteria. (was found)

New projects _____ every week in that class. (are/were/will be turned in)

Cell phones _____ every day. (are/were/will be used)

The children _____ not to play there. (were asked)

Jesus _____ by John. (was baptized)

A lot of classic cars _____ to that car show. (are/were/will be brought)

I _____ the good news yesterday. (was given)

Very expensive shoes _____ at that store. (are/were/will be sold)

That national park _____ by a lot of people. (is/was/will be loved)

The flowers _____ in the front garden. (are/were/will be planted)

A lot of pizza _____ every day at that cafe. (is/was/will be served)

The text message _____ two days ago. (was sent)

The package _____ before noon. (was/will be delivered)

Donated books _____ at the library weekly. (are/were/will be received)

Songs of praise _____ to God. (are/were/will be sung)

Two of every kind of animal _____ on the Ark. (were taken)

All the houses _____ white. (are/were/will be painted)

This car _____ last year. (was bought)

The temple _____ by King Solomon. (was built)

A cooking class _____ by Mrs. Rosso. (is/is being/was/will be taught)

THE Story of Easter

Appendix M

Reorder Sentences

Print one set of sentences for each group. Cut them apart along the dotted lines. Groups work together to reassemble the sentences in order. (Text is from Matthew 28:1–10.)

....

The Sabbath was over, and it was almost daybreak on Sunday when Mary Magdalene and the other Mary went to see the tomb.

....

Suddenly a strong earthquake struck, and the Lord's angel came down from heaven. He rolled away the stone and sat on it. The angel looked as bright as lightning, and his clothes were white as snow.

....

The guards shook from fear and fell down, as though they were dead. The angel said to the women, "Don't be afraid! I know you are looking for Jesus, who was nailed to a cross.

....

He isn't here! God has raised him to life, just as Jesus said he would. Come, see the place where his body was lying.

....

Now hurry! Tell his disciples he has been raised to life and is on his way to Galilee. Go there, and you will see him. This is what I came to tell you."

....

The women were frightened and yet very happy, as they hurried from the tomb and ran to tell his disciples. Suddenly Jesus met them and greeted them.

....

They went near him, held on to his feet, and worshiped him. Then Jesus said, "Don't be afraid! Tell my followers to go to Galilee. They will see me there."

....

ᴛʜᴇ Story of Easter
Appendix N
Lesson 19: Listening Comprehension

Choose the correct answer to finish each sentence.

1. The soldiers who had been guarding the tomb
   a. left the city to hide because they were afraid.
   b. went into the city.
   c. told the women to return to their homes.

2. They told the chief priests
   a. that they had finished their job and wanted to be paid.
   b. that they had fallen asleep on the job.
   c. everything that had happened.

3. The chief priests met with the leaders and decided to
   a. bribe the soldiers with a lot of money.
   b. punish the soldiers for letting the disciples steal the body.
   c. find the disciples to discover the truth.

4. The chief priests told the soldiers
   a. to leave the city and never return.
   b. to say that Jesus' disciples came during the night and stole the body.
   c. that they didn't believe their story of earthquakes and angels.

5. The soldiers
   a. refused the money because they would not lie.
   b. took the money and left for Rome.
   c. took the money and did what they were told.

Appendix N–Answers

1. The soldiers who had been guarding the tomb
   a. left the city to hide because they were afraid.
   b. went into the city.
   c. told the women to return to their homes.

2. They told the chief priests
   a. that they had finished their job and wanted to be paid.
   b. that they had fallen asleep on the job.
   c. everything that had happened.

3. The chief priests met with the leaders and decided to
   a. bribe the soldiers with a lot of money.
   b. punish the soldiers for letting the disciples steal the body.
   c. find the disciples to discover the truth.

4. The chief priests told the soldiers
   a. to leave the city and never return.
   b. to say that Jesus' disciples came during the night and stole the body.
   c. that they didn't believe their story of earthquakes and angels.

5. The soldiers
   a. refused the money because they would not lie.
   b. took the money and left for Rome.
   c. took the money and did what they were told.

THE Story of Easter

Appendix O

Lesson 20: Vocabulary Review

Use the clues to fill in the answers to this crossword puzzle with vocabulary words and phrases you have learned. If the answer is a phrase, there will be a space between the words.

Across

2. an occasion when people eat food together
5. to be in the right place; to feel happy or comfortable in a situation
6. use your hands to take somebody or something and hold it quickly or roughly
8. to annoy, worry, or upset someone
9. shows that every member of a group does something to or for the other members
10. to say unkind things about somebody so that other people will laugh at them

Down

1. to lift something to a higher position
3. a dream that is very frightening or unpleasant
4. opposing or disagreeing with somebody or something
7. to return to a place

Word Bank

each other	belong	meal	against
come back	bother	raise	grab
make fun	nightmare		

The Story of Easter

Lesson 20: Vocabulary Review

Use the clues to fill in the answers to this crossword puzzle with vocabulary words and phrases you have learned. If the answer is a phrase, there will be a space between the words.

Across

2. an occasion when people eat food together
5. to be in the right place; to feel happy or comfortable in a situation
6. use your hands to take somebody or something and hold it quickly or roughly
8. to annoy, worry, or upset someone
9. shows that every member of a group does something to or for the other members
10. to say unkind things about somebody so that other people will laugh at them

Down

1. to lift something to a higher position
3. a dream that is very frightening or unpleasant
4. opposing or disagreeing with somebody or something
7. to return to a place

Appendix O–Answers

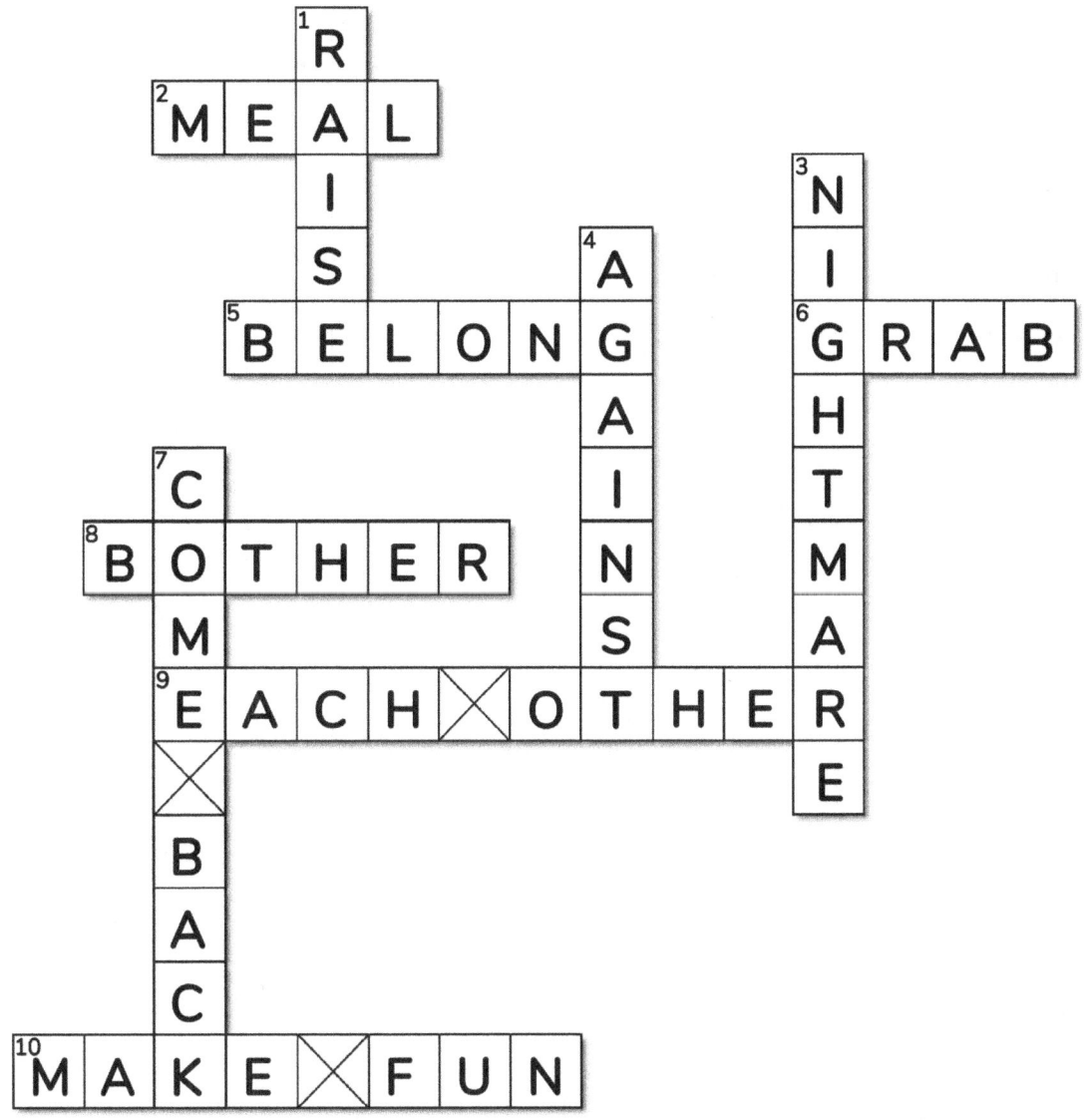

THE Story of Easter

Appendix P

Final Grammar Quiz

Part 1: Prepositions of Location: *In*, *On*, or *At*

Add the correct preposition of location to each blank: *in*, *on*, or *at*.

1. Minji is _____ the bus right now.
2. I'll see you _____ work on Monday.
3. He lives _____ Chicago.
4. Richard is working _____ his desk.
5. Marla has a cat _____ her lap.
6. Put the cookies _____ the oven.
7. Please pick me up _____ the airport.
8. I live (a) _____ an apartment (b) _____ Main Street.

Part 2: Prepositions *From* and *Of*

Choose the correct preposition for each blank: *from* or *of*.

1. The homework is due at the end _____ the week.
2. Jack is _____ New Orleans.
3. Has the bus _____ Newton arrived?
4. I bought five pounds _____ potatoes.
5. Those verses are _____ the Bible.
6. Jacob is a member _____ our team.
7. Jana and William live in the city _____ Dublin.
8. There is a crowd _____ people in the park.

Part 3: Prepositions of Time: *In, On, At,* or *During*

Add the correct preposition of time to each blank: *in, on, at,* or *during.*

1. We left the house _____ two o'clock.

2. Ebony was born _____ 1985.

3. We stayed in our seats _____ the whole performance.

4. There is a meeting _____ Sunday afternoon.

5. I have a doctor's appointment _____ Friday.

6. Easter is usually (a) _____ April, but sometimes it is (b) _____ March.

7. Please pick me up _____ noon.

8. I will be back _____ a few minutes.

Part 4: Prepositions *To, By, With, About,* and *As*

Choose the correct preposition for each blank: *to, by, with, about,* or *as.*

1. I'm worried _____ my friend. She hasn't called me this week.

2. Margareta lives _____ her parents.

3. We live in that house _____ the park.

4. Mr. and Mrs. Reyes are going _____ Paris next week.

5. You can use that old glass _____ a vase.

6. Did you hear _____ Maria's new job?

7. The dog likes to sleep _____ that old toy.

8. Let me explain it _____ you.

9. Be careful _____ Grandma's old dishes.

10. I was frightened _____ the noise.

11. That hamburger was as dry _____ the desert.

12. What are you talking _____ ?

Appendix P–Answers

Part 1: Prepositions of Location

1. Minji is <u>on</u> the bus right now.
2. I'll see you <u>at</u> work on Monday.
3. He lives <u>in</u> Chicago.
4. Richard is working <u>at</u> his desk.
5. Marla has a cat <u>on</u> her lap.
6. Put the cookies <u>in</u> the oven.
7. Please pick me up <u>at</u> the airport.
8. I live (a) <u>in</u> an apartment (b) <u>on</u> Main Street.

Part 2: Prepositions *From* and *Of*

1. The homework is due at the end <u>of</u> the week.
2. Jack is <u>from</u> New Orleans.
3. Has the bus <u>from</u> Newton arrived?
4. I bought five pounds <u>of</u> potatoes.
5. Those verses are <u>from</u> the Bible.
6. Jacob is a member <u>of</u> our team.
7. Jana and William live in the city <u>of</u> Dublin.
8. There is a crowd <u>of</u> people in the park.

Part 3: Prepositions of Time

1. We left the house <u>at</u> two o'clock.
2. Ebony was born <u>in</u> 1985.
3. We stayed in our seats <u>during</u> the whole performance.
4. There is a meeting <u>on</u> Sunday afternoon.
5. I have a doctor's appointment <u>on</u> Friday.
6. Easter is usually (a) <u>in</u> April, but sometimes it is (b) <u>in</u> March.
7. Please pick me up <u>at</u> noon.
8. I will be back <u>in</u> a few minutes.

Part 4: Prepositions *To, By, With, About,* and *As*

1. I'm worried <u>about</u> my friend. She hasn't called me this week.
2. Margareta lives <u>with</u> her parents.
3. We live in that house <u>by</u> the park.
4. Mr. and Mrs. Reyes are going <u>to</u> Paris next week.
5. You can use that old glass <u>as</u> a vase.
6. Did you hear <u>about</u> Maria's new job?
7. The dog likes to sleep <u>with</u> that old toy.
8. Let me explain it <u>to</u> you.
9. Be careful <u>with</u> Grandma's old dishes.
10. I was frightened <u>by</u> the noise.
11. That hamburger was as dry <u>as</u> the desert.
12. What are you talking <u>about</u>?

The Story of Easter

Appendix Q

Complete Vocabulary List

against–lesson 12
agreement–lesson 5
ahead–lesson 6
amazed–lesson 12
arrest–lesson 1
asleep–lesson 19
betray–lesson 3
bitterly–lesson 10
blessed–lesson 5
bother–lesson 2
bribe–lesson 19
bright–lesson 18
bring–lesson 12
carry–lesson 15
certain–lesson 4
chance–lesson 3
charges–lesson 12
chief–lesson 3
claim–lesson 17
coins–lesson 3
convince–lesson 13
courtyard–lesson 9
curtain–lesson 16
daybreak–lesson 18
desert–lesson 16
deserve–lesson 9
during–lesson 5
each other–lesson 19
even–lesson 10
forgiven–lesson 5
free (verb)–lesson 13
grab–lesson 16
greet–lesson 8
guard–lesson 19

home–lesson 4
kneel–lesson 14
meal–lesson 5
mob–lesson 8
nail–lesson 1
nightmare–lesson 13
(his) own–lesson 15
Passover–lesson 1
place–lesson 14
poor–lesson 2
pot–lesson 11
pour–lesson 2
prepare–lesson 4
pretend–lesson 14
raise–lesson 6
refuse–lesson 15
reject–lesson 6
rest (of)–lesson 14
riot–lesson 1
roll–lesson 17
scatter–lesson 6
seal–lesson 17
shake–lesson 18
simply–lesson 7
sneak–lesson 1
soak–lesson 16
surely–lesson 4
thin–lesson 4
troubled–lesson 7
trust–lesson 15
turn (become)–lesson 16
waste–lesson 2
world–lesson 2
wrap–lesson 17

Expressions and Idioms

a little while–lesson 10
a thing–lesson 12
at last–lesson 9
even though–lesson 9
how much–lesson 3
make fun (of)–lesson 14
on (their) way–lesson 19
right up–lesson 8
take the blame–lesson 13
that isn't so–lesson 10

Phrasal verbs

be over–lesson 18
belong to–lesson 11
come back–lesson 7
come to–lesson 15
come up–lesson 10
come together–lesson 13
go away–lesson 17
go over–lesson 7
hand over–lesson 1
hold on–lesson 18
lead away–lesson 11
pick up–lesson 11
pull out–lesson 8
put away–lesson 8
strike down–lesson 6
take along–lesson 7
tear down–lesson 9
tie up–lesson 11

"Here is the Lamb of God who takes away
the sin of the world!"

~John the Baptist, John 1:29

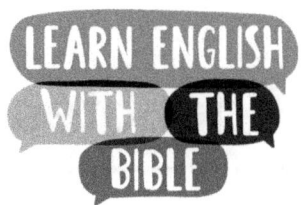

I hope this Bible-based English course highlighting prepositions is helpful, informative, and useful for you and your students. More importantly, I hope the lessons have provided another way for you to reach out to people in your community with the gospel.

I would love to hear about your ministry, your ideas, and how I can be of more help to you. Soon there will be other materials available on the website for future classes.

Your feedback is important to me. I'd love for you to send me comments about what your students enjoyed, what activities worked well for you and your group, and parts of the Bible that you would like me to cover in the next course. Write to me at: sharon@learnenglishwiththebible.com.

I wish you all the best and God's blessings as you show your care and concern for people by sharing the gospel of Christ.

In Him,

Sharon

❧ Endnotes ❧

1. "The Truth about 'Y': It's Mostly a Vowel." Merriam-Webster Dictionary online. Accessed July 2023. merriam-webster.com/words-at-play/why-y-is-sometimes-a-vowel-usage.

2. "Rachel's English: Ben Franklin Exercises," archive of past lessons. Accessed July 2023. https://rachelsenglish.com/tag/ben-franklin-exercises/.

3. "English Pronunciation of 'What.'" Accessed May 2, 2023. https://dictionary.cambridge.org/us/pronunciation/english/what.

4. "Pronunciation of 'what' pronoun," *Oxford Learner's Dictionaries*, Accessed July 2023. https://www.oxfordlearnersdictionaries.com/us/definition/english/what?q=what.

5. "Definition of 'miracle' noun," *Oxford Learner's Dictionaries*, Accessed July 2023. https://www.oxfordlearnersdictionaries.com/us/definition/english/miracle?q=miracle.

6. "Preposition List," English CLUB. Accessed July 2023. https://www.englishclub.com/grammar/prepositions-list.php.